TCHOTCHKES

Budlong Woods Writers

D1318346

TCHOTCHKES

Budlong Woods Writers

Cover Photo courtesy of Richard Kimball
Cover Design courtesy of Carol Beu
Photographs and original art courtesy of Elizabeth Barton, Carol Beu, Daniel Cleary, Enid Fefer, Daelyn Frasier, Richard Kimball, Donna Pecore, Tony Pigott, Tom Stark and Robynne Wallace
Book Design courtesy of Carol Beu, Donna Pecore
Editors, Elizabeth Barton Judy Soohoo and Ann Fiegen.

DPOETRAE PRODUCTIONS 2019

This book was made possible with the support of the Chicago Public Library, specifically the Budlong Woods Branch head librarian, Thomas Stark. Our roots are found in the philosophy of the late organization, the Neighborhood Writing Alliance, where "Everyone is a philosopher and has something to say." Also, offering gratitude to Janise Hurtig of the Community Writing Project who shared Popular Education's process and facilitator training. Which brings us to the Budlong Woods Writers, without whom there would be no beautiful book. They generously shared their words, art, and time, some weekly, culminating in this galvanizing collection.

ISBN: 9781702788823

Produced with Kindle Printing, a division of Amazon.

CONTENTS

INTRODUCTION

Donna Pecore

Tchotchke

A small piece of worthless crap, a decorative knickknack with little or no purpose. Side note: It can be pretty, sentimental, or even occasionally useful, although it usually breaks easily if useful. If you are having trouble identifying Tchotchkes, just look around your house or someone else's and whatever you see that a burglar wouldn't steal is probably a Tchotchke.
Urban Dictionary by Robin and Stephany October 31, 2007

You're wondering about the title, so I offer this definition, and proceed to bloviate a bit about my favorite subjects, the work of the Budlong writers and writing and words. You might think it is a little crass referring to this, their book, a thing of worthless crap, but the odds and ends of life are here. What one values and collects, refusing to let go of for no reason but one's own. The stories inside are the beautiful and the ugly knickknacks that have caught our eyes and captured our hearts. You may find value here or you may just find this collection curious, but this anthology is definitely worth adding to your collection of Tchotchkes.

The writers in here are no nincompoops, they are erudite and thinkers, some followed the prompt and others went their own way. I made no brouhaha over their lack of cooperation nor entered into a donnybrook with them, but let them write what they wished. What was produced in group may not be representative of theme but represents what I could not let go of, so these grabbers are included here. The intrinsic value of a piece (writing or knickknack) is based on the joy it brings. I give you a gadyloo, this book is full of gubbins and may, unintentionally, give you the collywobbles.

Participants come from the neighborhood and all corners of the city, no taradiddles with snickersnees, just nice people with widershins of perspectives. This is not a lot of malarkey, but a challenge for you to get in the front row and feel a little sialoquent. And please pardon my facetiousness.

No borborygm, just get your dictionary out to enjoy these little Tchotchkes of mine. The unique and crazy words that tickle ears and bring joy to hearts. Apologies for not being pauciloquent, just xertz and dig-in, you may find ratoons, things to grow some thoughts. Don't be afraid to bibble and you will wish you started reading this anthology nudiustertian. So no more lollygagging or you'll look like a rolled up erinaceous.

Enough from this ol' snollygoster, get your guire on and if you are lazy and in a bumfuzzle you don't need a bumbershoot for the load of crap dropped on you, just go to Expresswriters.com and check out the article, *34 of the Craziest Words in English*, or aka, one of my personal knickknack shelves. (How many words did I use? And, how many did you look up?) Enjoy the Budlong Writer's Tchotchkes! P.S. Does anyone know where to get a flaming flamingo hat? I need a little whimsy.

Ballad of the Tchotchkes with Moxie

Tim Andersen

I said, "Hello" to Golden Plate.
"How was hibernation?"
"It sucked," sneered Plate. "What took so long?
That's too much vacation."

Saucer spoke. He said, "Why?
Your parents loved us dearly."
"They're dead," I said. "I packed you up.
I took you home. The in-laws nearly

sold you." But Cup was having none
of it. His language was R rated.
Suffice to say my ears were burned.
My choices were berated.

Cup swore some more. If Cup had hair
it surely would have bristled.
"What happened to our shelf mates?
The Beer Mugs and the Crystal?"

"They're in the kitchen on a shelf.
They don't get used too often.
Dad's favorite Mug—the German one—
went into his coffin."

"Oh no you didn't! What an asshole!"
That did not go well.
Then Lladro, Vase and Bakelite
started raising holy hell.

Fiestaware, Pottery
Hummel Figurines,
Coffee Grinder, Glassware
and Mini Tambourines

were harping, carping, barking and snarking,
all adding to the fray
until I commandeered their box
and loudly shouted. "Hey!

Guess what," I said. "You're not in charge.
I'm sealing you back up.
I'll see you in a year or two
and then I'm selling Cup."

Love

Tim Andersen

When love is crystalline it is most obscure,
its aspect framed by a grey burnish
plunging in a downward spiral
outside the porthole of a tramp steamer at sunset.

Its existence grabs distance
and yanks it closer as it drifts further away
toward a numberless accuracy
comprehensible as a hue but
incomprehensible as a color.

Its existence offers darkened corners
maneuvering close and away
from a midpoint of lingering possibility.

An arrangement with Waterloo recognizes the gravity
of venturing forth. Mortality shows up at the door
and gains admittance

but the termination of love is worse,
a void brimming with gloom
shoving its way toward an uncourageous lit-up ache,
a sooty exterior of botched allness.

Love is the stuff that nature makes ill.
It tastes terrible sometimes
but it's good medicine,
a dusty glow that leaves a residue
on the inside of the person
inside the house,
blurting as only it can.

Hurricane

Tim Andersen

Yowzer!

My house just blew away
from Hurricane Irma. Katrina.

Divas at a fever pitch.
Dive into a ditch.

Keith got hit
in the teeth
by a flying bi-valve.

Don't buy a house
in New Orleans
just rent.

The money spent
day by day
on your house
with your spouse

could all just go away
from Hurricane Joe Moe Rita Frieda
Ann Fran Bill Phil. Pick your poison pill.

Uh-oh! Here comes Joe.
He's the boss of the Red Cross.
He stammers yammers mansplains
on and on and on.

Here comes Biff. He's the stiff
from FEMA. Biff and Joe don't get along.
There is pee upon each other's pants
about who knows more than what.

Luckily, their bosses called them in.
They left and left behind
the bane of our existence.

The weather falls and the forecast calls
for us to confront that front

building up to the south
swirling as a clockwise
motion in the ocean.

See That Guy Over There?

Tim Andersen

I know him // He is still slim / and trim // Back in the day he was buff / stuff // He had the tannest / tan / and the blondest / blonde hair / on Oak Street Beach //

When we were in Dodge / College / he got the football team as high / as blue cheese in the sky / the night before a game / and the next day / we won anyway //

He was the oldest guy in school // One day he skipped / wrestling practice / He had to buy beer / for some fraternity mucky mucks / who paid him fifty bucks // The coach called him a turd / and a shitbird / but did not kick him off the team // Coach / wanted to catch / him red-handed with beer / so he could hand down something more severe //

Coach never did catch him // After college / he signed with an agency / scored some commercials / got bit parts on TV shows / then got into two movies / and won some obscure award / for one of them // The arc of his success was ridiculous //

And it was only because he was / stupid / handsome / like a cartoon character version of handsome // So he goes on stage to get his award / and a woman who looks like a goddess / hands him his trophy and he kisses it / and in his speech he seems sincere / but he has been practicing graceful self-effacement / which makes him ideal for promoting / manly skin care products //

He has the finesse the monarchs of manipulation / made for him // He is awesome /
write the worshipers // His preeminent bro mist / coils around / a resounding providential calibration / of scintillating magnitude / at least until tomorrow / next week / next month

Photo by Carol Beu

So Cool
(a sestina)

Tim Andersen

One day I
decided to be bold and wear
gold
shoes with red
trim. I looked so cool
I wore them to bed.

I decided to be bold in bed
so I
bought cool
sleepwear—
red
and gold

pajamas with matching gold
condoms on the nightstand by the bed.
I also bought a small red
lava lamp for atmosphere and I
swear
it was so cool.

What else was so cool
was this Russian gold
chain that I bought for a song and wear
all the time except to bed.
I
use it as a bookmark. I'm well read

you know. I used to have red
sheets. They were so cool
but died of old age. I
saw a set with gold
pinstripes, perfect in my new bedroom full of jewelry, shoes and sleepwear.

I used to never wear
pink or red.
I dressed bland to blend in. My bed-
room was white, and my shoes were black. Not cool.
My new look is a new man because I wear
gold and red
in my cool bed.

mrandersen and his Flamingo Hat

Tim Andersen

There's mrandersen
He wears a flamingo hat
He scares the neighborhood children

The neighbors called a meeting
What are we going to do about
mrandersen's hat

Some of the neighborhood women
said mrandersen? he's ok

But the women vetting mrandersen
had no clout

The moms called the cops
who asked What's this about?

He's scaring out children
with his flamingo hat

The cops asked Why are you
wearing that flamingo hat

Artistic expression
said mrandersen

The cops were flummoxed
1st amendment rights
vs neighborhood moms

The cops sided with the moms
because there were a lot them
but there was only one
mrandersen

The cops told him to take off his hat
mrandersen said It's a hat

The cops took his hat off for him
and shoved it in his chest
and told him to get lost

Tim Andersen has published poems in many magazines over the last 45 years and has self-published two books: Jet Plane and Nine. Besides reading and writing, Tim likes to cook, play bridge, and bowl. His waggish wit delights the Budlong Woods writers.

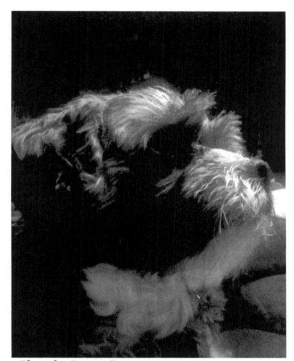

Photo by Donna Pecore

Photo by Robynne Wallace

The Joy of Socks

Elizabeth Barton

It's time for me to admit I have a problem. In the grand scheme of things, it's not a terrible problem, but I can't ignore it anymore, so I'm going to own up. If I have been even moderately diligent about keeping up with the laundry, my sock drawer is overstuffed to the point that I can't fully close it. The issue actually first reared its head a few years ago when I was keeping my socks and my tights in a single drawer—that this was once possible seems amazing to me now. I deferred the problem by transferring my tights to a storage box that now sits beside my dresser. Alas, that too is now overflowing. In the interest of full disclosure, I should also mention that holiday/season-themed socks (e.g., those depicting pumpkins, witches, reindeer, snowflakes, and the like) are kept in separate storage and unearthed when seasonally appropriate.

I don't recall exactly when my sock preoccupation (or presockupation as I have come to call it) began. I didn't just wake up one day, suddenly sock crazed. I don't remember being particularly sock focused in my younger days. I had the basic neutrals—black, navy, grey, brown—and I usually had a few pairs with stripes, argyle, or polka dots to jazz things up. Occasionally, as a gift I'd receive a pair with something a little nuttier, like a zebra print. At the time I probably wouldn't have thought to buy such socks for myself, but those gifts would always bring a smile to my face. I think that was when I started to get hooked.

A dozen or so years ago, I was in Target (a perilous place, a veritable minefield for anyone with even the slightest tendency to make impulse purchases) when I spotted a pair of socks on an end-of-aisle display. Their predominant pattern was black and grey stripes, but these weren't simple straight stripes. Rather, they were somewhat curvy and irregular, like the stripes of a tabby cat. Up at the top of the socks were adorable cat faces, one on each sock. I stopped for a moment, smiled, and continued on with my shopping excursion. Yet, as I got my vitamins, conditioner, and laundry detergent, my mind returned to the socks. They were kind of perfect. Most people would just see the stripes, which were kind of funky but still basically neutral-colored stripes. But above those stripes, hidden by the sock-wearer's pants, the cute silly kitty faces would lurk in covert whimsy.

Eventually, I had made a loop around the store and was back near the socks. I paused for a second but passed them by again. Nah, I don't need them, I told myself as I headed toward the checkout counters. I was kidding myself. After about fifteen paces, I turned abruptly, went back, and grabbed the socks.

Those were my gateway socks. I began a wild ride down the slippery slope of sock addiction, which happened to coincide with an explosion in the whimsical sock industry—or so it seemed. Perhaps an endless array of kooky sock options had always been available, but I hadn't noticed. Quickly, I began to realize that, for any aspect of my personality I wished to express, there was a corresponding pair of socks. For instance, if you didn't know I was a writer, you might figure it out by looking at my feet on any given day because I have socks with motifs of typewriters, pencils, books, and library cards. I have one pair where one sock has the full titles of once-banned books and the other has the titles blacked out, as if they had been attacked by a censor with a thick marker. I've got socks from New York, Paris, Amsterdam, Alaska, Hawaii, Napa, and Dublin. I was dismayed to come home from a recent trip without having found a pair of Luxembourg-themed socks. I have socks with hot air balloons, wine bottles, musical notes, galaxies, narwhals, and Rosie the Riveter. I even have a pair of socks with pictures of shoes on them. Ironically, I don't have any sock-print socks, but I have no doubt that such things exist. I've got socks with colorful patterns along with fun sayings like "Duchess of Sassytown" and "Let's carpe the fuck out of this diem." I have three pairs of socks that identify me as a badass. Shortly after I was diagnosed with breast cancer, a friend bought me a pair of hot pink socks that depict a purple cat flipping the bird and proclaiming, "Fuck cancer!" I wore those socks for every one of my chemo treatments.

Even with my wide and varied collection, I know I've barely begun to scratch the surface of the novelty footwear world. I've learned that there are at least ten different sock subscriptions services, and although I have not (yet) joined any of them, it feels good to know they're out there. It lets me know I'm not alone in my presock-upation. Frankly, as addictions go, this one is fairly benign, but, as they say, admitting you have a problem is the first step in dealing with it. So, yes, I admit it. I have a problem: I need a bigger dresser.

Photo by Daelyn Frasier

I Am From

Elizabeth Barton

I am from all-copper pre-1982 pennies
saved in large coffee cans
from Noxzema and mosquito punk sticks
I'm from a bedroom with lime-green shag carpet
yellow and white gingham wallpaper
(décor so loud it's a wonder I could sleep)

I am from maple tree helicopters
and towering spruces
in whose branches at night
I swore I could see the face of a witch
I am from Saturday morning cartoons
and Sunday morning pancakes

I am from frugality and laughter
from a farm-boy dad and a city-girl mom
who raised small-town kids
I am from sweet corn
and homemade chocolate chip cookies

I am from Jeepers cats! and Are we having fun yet?
from the Golden Rule and Think for yourself
I'm from ribboned barrettes and friendship pins
from roller-skates and saucer sleds
snow forts and Big Wheels

I am from trips to the beach with Grandma and cousins
Jolly Good soda for all
a T-shirt over my bathing suit as SPF
I'm from summer road-trip family vacations
in a car with no a/c
(on one trip I got chicken pox)

My mother lovingly pried fading photos
from self-adhesive albums
whose glue was now brittle
scanned each one into bits and bytes
Digitally preserved memories

My brother and I time-travel
traversing decades over cocktails
and conversations
where every sentence seems to begin
Remember that time...

How Are You?

Elizabeth Barton

People ask me this frequently. To be clear, I'm not talking about the congenial but perfunctory inquiries of grocery store cashiers or baristas, voiced mainly out of habit or a need to fill silence. The queries I refer to come from people I know, some from acquaintances, others from close friends and even family members. I have several stock answers.

- I'm hanging in there
- Could be better, could be worse
- OK...considering

These responses might not provide a lot of information, but they have to suffice because really answering the question is way too complicated. It would take a long time, and I don't think it's what people really want when they ask. It's not that I suspect people ask about my well-being only to be polite—I do think they are genuinely concerned about my condition. It's just that they want the Cliff's Notes version of the answer, which is fine because usually, neither they nor I have time for more. So, I usually give one of my canned responses. It's easier. Besides, when it really comes down answering the question How are you? the truth is, I just don't know.

In many ways, my day-to-day life hasn't changed since I was diagnosed with breast cancer. My time is still filled with work, household chores, and hobbies. Granted, I rest more often, and in any given week, I almost always have at least one appointment with some doctor or another. I don't look that much different. My wig resembles my pre-cancer hair reasonably well, and I didn't lose weight on chemotherapy like a lot of people do. There are a few differences, though. I often look tired, and I feel like this whole thing has aged me, but then again, I started out looking young for my age, so I guess I've got that going for me. If you look closely, you might notice my eyebrows are drawn on since my real ones have become quite sparse. The biggest differences, though, are not obvious to the casual observer. I'm not talking about the physical effects of the cancer itself or the gallons of poison I had pumped into my veins during months of chemotherapy. Neither am I referring to scars from biopsies and surgery. I'm talking about the mental differences.

When I think back, even though it was only about six months ago, my pre-cancer life seems like a different planet—one I wish I could visit, if only for a little while, a vacation from cancer if you will. The first few weeks after I got the news were a frenzied haze of disbelief, anger, and fear. I wondered if there would ever again come a time when I wasn't terrified all the time. Thankfully, that changed as I received more information, a prognosis, and a treatment plan. After some of the initial fear subsided, I was revved up and ready to fight. I couldn't wait to start treatment—I was going to kick the shit out of this thing that was trying to take over my body.

Chemo was rough. Really rough. At times it seemed endless. But before long, I could literally feel my tumor shrinking, and I clung to that knowledge when I was feeling my worst. I sometimes wonder what I would have done, how I would have felt if I hadn't known the chemo was working. On top of the fatigue, the nausea, the hair loss, the blisters on my hands and feet, and the fact that everything tasted off, what if I also had to deal with constant paralyzing fear like what I'd felt just after my diagnosis? How would I handle that? I guess I'd find a way because it's not like there's an alternative. Several people remarked about how brave I've been through all of this, but I don't see it that way. I've simply been playing with the hand I was dealt. I haven't endured chemotherapy and surgery out of courage, just out of necessity. My sense of self-preservation kicked in and keeps me going, even though the uncertainty of the future I'm heading toward scares the hell out of me. At this point, I'm reasonably confident that I still have a long life ahead of me, but I feel like I can't conjure a clear picture of what that life might look like, which is s scary in its own way. I'm pretty sure my life will never be the same as before I was diagnosed. Some things will seemingly return to normal. My hair is starting to grow back, slowly but surely. Some day, I'll have real eyebrows again. The sutures from my surgery will heal, and the scars will grow fainter over time. For a while, a daily commute to receive radiation therapy will become my new normal, and after that, I'll have years of anti-hormone therapy and whatever side effects accompany that. But I wonder, if and when all this is over and I beat this thing, who will I be without cancer?

On some level, I know I'm much more than my cancer, but it's so easy to lose sight of that when something takes over your life the way an illness like this tends to. Certainly, having it take over my life beats the hell out of having it take my life, but it's scary not knowing what the future will look like. Will my identity shift from cancer patient to cancer survivor? In forming our identities, we choose some things—writer, vegetarian, cat person, knitter, Cubs fan. For others, we have no choice in the matter, and sometimes those shift abruptly, like when I found myself going from healthy woman in the prime of her life to cancer patient in the blink of an eye. I certainly never wanted to define myself by a disease, but cancer is insidious. It has a way of creeping in, inserting itself into your identity, much like the malignant tumor proliferates and displaces healthy tissue. You hate it, but it's a part of you, and even if you think it's all been cut out, there could still be small bits of it lying in wait. Imagining life without cancer becomes almost as difficult as wrapping your mind around your own death. Ostensibly, it would be just like before you were born, but somehow, it just doesn't compute.

So, how am I? It's just so hard to say. Perhaps it's too soon to tell. Maybe I should just give one of my stock responses and not think about it too much while I simply continue to play the cards I've been dealt. That's all any of us can really do.

12

The Ballad of Belle Gunness

Elizabeth Barton

`Norwegian-born near Selbu Lake in 1859
Although she came from modest means, Belle grew robust and fine
In 1881 she crossed the ocean with desire
To find wealth in America, to lead a life less dire
Chicago-bound was this young belle; there Sorenson she wed
They opened up a little store, sold sweetmeats, ginger bread
Alas, a fire destroyed the shop, which had not seen success
Insurance payout saved the day! For Belle was truly blessed
A happy pair they must have been 'til some years later on
One summer's day, he met his end, Belle's dear Sorenson
Cause of death: his heart had failed, though some declared foul play
They said that Belle with strychnine had put Sorenson away
The timing of her husband's death it seems was just too apt
Twice-insured he died the day those policies o'erlapped

But Belle unscathed, no charges filed, she took her windfall dough
She moved to Indiana next and found a brand new beau
The widower Pete Gunness soon made Belle his blushing bride
But happy times turned sorrowful when Pete's young daughter died
And such bad luck, more came so soon, just eight months down the line
Poor Pete met an accident—was burnt by scalding brine
To make things worse, some heavy gear from on a nearby ledge
Crashed down on Pete and hit his head, or so Belle did allege
This time folks just would not buy the tale that Belle had spun
Demanded further inquiry so justice could be done
The coroner reviewed the case, and murder he decreed
But crafty Belle convinced the cops that she'd done no misdeed
Some years passed uneventfully, on second thought, not quite
Belle's foster daughter Jennie seemed to disappear from sight
Belle said she went off to school, although this was a lie
The truth remained a secret, which I'll tell you by and by

In time, it seems Belle got to be quite lonesome on her farm
She cast a net through personal ads to emphasize her charm
Comely widow seeks to meet a gentleman upright
With view of joining fortunes, thus in marriage to unite
Glib responses Belle insisted she'd not dignify
She stated this quite plainly so: Triflers need not apply
And suitors soon began to come from places far and near
To win Belle's hand, to demonstrate intentions so sincere
One named John arrived to prove he'd outdo other men
Within a week, he disappeared, was never seen again
No one can say with confidence how many came to call

We might in fact need several extra hands to count them all
A man whose name was Anderson was lucky you might say
For he alone escaped Belle's trap—the one who got away

Meanwhile Belle did curious things; she ordered hefty trunks
So many it's unlikely they were just for storing junk
What then could their purpose be, and might that be connected
To tales that some began to tell of sights quite unexpected?
Folks passing by the farm at night had claimed they'd spotted Belle
In the hog pen toiling, digging, why they could not tell
Still all the while more suitors flocked; one from Wisconsin came
A well-appointed widower; Budsberg was his name
Last seen alive inside a bank obtaining wads of cash
And signing over deeds to land—an act some thought quite rash
In time his children worried, wondered, wrote to Belle, inquired
Had their father been to visit? If so, what had transpired?
Belle's letter of reply composed, and it was quickly sent
With deep regret she told the children she'd not seen this gent

We can't forget Ray Lamphere—hired hand on Belle's estate
With Belle he grew quite smitten, and his jealousy was great
When callers came to visit Belle, he'd get in quite a snit
At last one day Belle fired him, saying he was most unfit
But Lamphere would not stay away; Belle said he caused her strife
She told anyone who'd listen then that she feared for her life
And rightly so perhaps, you see, for late one April night
The Gunness house was claimed by fire, burning fierce and bright
A body in the ruins lay, found absent of its head
Even so, townsfolk assumed that Belle was surely dead
And Lamphere was the culprit; he'd clearly set the blaze
So he would sit in prison the remainder of his days

All around much gossip spread, and rumors they did fly
About the things that might be buried out in Belle's hog sty
And when police began to search, what ghastly things they found!
Bodies, some in parts, some whole, buried underground
Perhaps a dozen, maybe more, there were so very many
And as you may have guessed by now, indeed, they found poor Jennie
You might think it served Belle right to burn up like she had
Not so I fear! For I have just a little more to add
Exactly what became of Belle, no one can say for sure
But that body in the ashes found, we now know was not her
Although that corpse was badly burned and lacking head and neck
Its measurements did not fit Belle's when someone thought to check
There long persisted gossip of Belle sightings far and wide
Quite tantalizing rumors, yes, but never verified

We'll never know with certainty the number that Belle killed
Some put the total over forty graves this wily woman filled
It seems unjust that such an awful villain got away
Then again, by now she's dead I think it's safe to say
But let us not take too much peace and comfort in that thought
Mankind it seems has endless stores of evil to be fought

Photo by Carol Beu

Crossroads?
(A Golden Shovel Poem)

Elizabeth Barton

I cannot help but think, has it come to this?
Are these strange times an omen, cryptic as it is?
Could this turn of events finally be the
indisputable evidence that we the people have lost our way?
Or might it instead be something more uncertain, the
proverbial turning point that will seal the fate of the world?
For better or worse, will we find that the ends
do indeed justify the means, although it may not
be apparent as we live in the moment, laden with
so much turmoil, confusion, and injustice looming in a
stifling cloud? We feel powerless do anything but bang
our heads against metaphorical walls. But
still, somehow, all the while, we continue to harbor a
quiet sliver of hope, even as we whimper.

"This is the way the world ends
Not with a bang but a whimper"
—From The Hollow Men by T. S. Elliot

Elizabeth Barton is a lifelong logoleptic (i.e., word nerd). She has been writing since she was a child, and, for almost as long, she's been making up excuses for not having written more. She occasionally blogs at lizardesque.wordpress.com. Undoubtedly, she would blog a lot more and might even be a famous, best-selling author by now if she didn't get so distracted by her hobby of collecting hobbies (e.g., photography, ceramics, knitting, yoga, puzzle-solving, and, most recently, learning to play ukulele). Elizabeth enjoys non sequiturs, and her name anagrams to brazen albeit hot and blaze into breath.

Prayer

Carol Beu

It was a summer day in 2018 when I walked into the room that housed a new exhibit at the Art Institute of Chicago. The room was long and narrow, approximately 80 by 24 feet. The ceiling appeared to be 16 feet high. Three of the walls were a stark white. The fourth wall was floor-to-ceiling glass windows. Outside, a steady rain was pouring down on the patio. A museum guard stood quietly by the door.

The exhibit, Prayer, was the work of James Webb, a South African artist. He first created and displayed the piece in 2000 in Cape Town. Just five years after the end of apartheid, he'd wanted to find a way to connect the people of his country and chanced upon the idea for this exhibit. Since then he'd been invited nine times to bring this healing work to other cities around the world. This was the tenth and largest presentation of Prayer to date.

Though large, the installation was surprisingly simple—some people have described it as "minimalist." A bright red carpet ran nearly the length of the room. A dozen round black objects were scattered across the center of the carpet. Closer inspection revealed that these objects were actually speakers and that voices—singing, speaking—were coming from each of them. The sounds blended together, and the overall effect was a confusing cacophony of sound—a virtual Tower of Babel.

The guard invited me to remove my shoes and walk onto the carpet to get closer to the speakers. She suggested that I lean in or sit down beside them. Upon doing so, I began to hear the individual speakers and realized that prayers and hymns—some in English, some in other languages—came from each. Moving from speaker to speaker, the sounds changed. The prayers and hymns that I was hearing were collected by Mr. Webb in answer to his question, "What would it be like to hear the prayers of an entire city simultaneously?" During the past summer, he had gone to over a hundred churches, temples, and mosques in Chicagoland. He'd recorded 250 people, clergy and laity alike, as they offered up prayers for peace and the well-being of their fellow humans.
I must have spent over 15 minutes moving about and listening to the offerings from each speaker. As I progressed, I found that I would kneel over each speaker, truly a prayerful position. I could have spent much longer—there were actually nine hours of recordings to be heard—but my knees began to offer up prayers of their own. So I stood up and stepped back. The beautiful prayers receded back into the uniform blur of sound that I'd heard upon first entering the exhibit. The sounds were quietly insistent and, in a way, somewhat annoying.

"Is this what God hears?" I thought. "All of us sending up our prayers and petitions?" I looked at the guard and said, "This must drive God crazy."

She smiled and agreed that it could be irritating. She admitted that she hadn't known how she would handle it when she was first assigned to the exhibit. "But I got used to it," she said. "And now I rather like it."

She also told me that one of the other guards who works with her loved it from the start. "It's so relaxing!" the woman exclaimed. She just loved working the exhibit. Eventually she started to bring socks from home so that she could loan them to museum goers who weren't wearing any and didn't want to walk on the carpet barefoot.

I had to laugh out loud at this! Such a simple, unexpected act of kindness. We all long to make the world a better place. Sometimes we offer up prayers for peace. We lend our support to people and organizations we think are doing good in the world. We wonder about that grand gesture that would bring us the miracle of healing for our planet. But what if it's not any of those? What if it's that small act of kindness that has the power to lift us up and make us whole? What if it's offering socks to strangers that has the power to save us?

And so, with those many thoughts and questions in my mind, I put on my shoes and left the exhibit.

Photo by Donna Pecore

The Blizzard of '67

Carol Beu

Thursday, January 26, 1967. It began to snow at 5:02 am. No big deal there—after all, it was Chicago. The weather forecasters had predicted we would get four inches of snow. What made it truly spectacular and memorable was the fact that by the time the snow stopped at 10:00 am the following day, we had a whopping 23 inches of snow on the ground—the largest single snowfall in the city's history.

On that day, I was a newlywed living on the north side of the city and working 11 miles out in the suburbs at a Sears store. On Thursdays, I worked the early shift, from 9:00 am to 5:30 pm. Frankly, I don't remember much about my drive to work. It started out like any other snowy day in Chicago—put on your boots and coat, brush the snow off your car, climb in, and very carefully drive down the street.

Something must be understood here, though. In 1967, long before satellite data and supercomputers made snow forecasting a relatively accurate process, the actual weather rarely matched what the forecasters predicted. These days we expect to know what the weather will be, when it will arrive, and how long it will last. But on that day, nobody—not the experts, not the average citizens—expected what was about to happen.

By noon, we had passed the four inches that had been predicted, and the snow was coming down fast and furious, showing no signs of stopping. The few customers who came to the store in the morning had fled for home, and the sales staff was left anxiously staring out the doors and imagining their homebound commute. By 3:00 pm management announced that anyone who wished to do so was free to leave. I gratefully took them up on this offer, grabbed my coat, and headed out to my car.

By that time, the parking lot was deep in snow, and I had to wait for nearly an hour for a mall plow to clear a path from my parking space out to the street. It took nearly three hours, but eventually I made it to the street I lived on and discovered that, not surprisingly, it had not been plowed. I made it exactly one block and was then stopped by the snow and cars blocking the street. The snow was knee-deep, but I somehow made it on foot to my door.

Upon awakening the next morning, we knew that, like most of the people in the city, we were stranded and would not be getting to work. Most of the day was spent watching reports of the storm on TV and heading outside to join our neighbors in shoveling out our parking lot and the street where our cars were stranded.

And that's when I began to focus on my next challenge. Unlike so many people who had the weekend off and could relax for a couple more days, I had to be at my job on Saturday morning. Saturday is always an important day in retail, but that particular Saturday was the most important day in the retail year. That Saturday was the day of the annual inventory—the day when all of the merchandise in the store was counted. It was the day that determines whether the previous year, with all of its sales activities, has proved profitable or not. So important was that day that nobody was allowed to have the day off. Unless you had a note from your doctor certifying that there was a major medical emergency, you had to be there. You could be fired if you did not show up.

At that point, my car was still stranded in a snowdrift in the middle of the street. So, I needed to figure out another way to get to work. I formulated this plan: I could walk the two blocks to Peterson Avenue, where I could catch a bus that would take me to the intersection of Caldwell and Central Avenues. From there, it was approximately a one-mile walk along Devon Avenue through the forest preserve to Milwaukee Avenue, where I could catch another bus that would take me to the shopping center. I wasn't thrilled at the prospect of doing this, but couldn't think of any other options.

So, on Saturday morning, I set off from my apartment, carrying a small suitcase loaded with stuff I would need in case I ended up spending the night in the store. I walked down to Peterson Avenue and was relieved to see that it had been plowed and traffic seemed to be moving smoothly.

There were several people waiting for the bus. And that's what we did. We waited. And waited. And waited with no sign of a bus. As we waited, people driving by would stop and offer a lift to the people on the curb. Several of the people I was standing with took the drivers up on these offers, but I was too well versed in the dangers of hitchhiking to join them. But as the time went by, the offers became more appealing. After all, I didn't know if a bus was ever going to come. And today was a special situation, wasn't it? These people were just being neighborly, weren't they? So eventually, I decided that I was going to get into the next car that stopped and offered a lift.

Eventually, a car did pull up to the curb, and the driver opened the door and shouted merrily, "Hop in!" So I, along with four other people piled into the car. I happily settled into the back seat and began to listen to conversations around me. Slowly it began to dawn on me. This wasn't the polite conversation of strangers. These people knew each other! It was some kind of a carpool, and I had forced my way into their midst! I was totally mortified. So at the next corner, I said something like, "This is my stop," and tried to make as graceful an exit from the car as possible.

Thus, I found myself, yet again, standing on a street corner, waiting for a bus that might never come. It was then that I reviewed my predicament. I had made it part of the way to work by essentially hitchhiking. Nothing bad had happened. Perhaps I could get myself to work (or at least to the next bus) by hitchhiking. And that's exactly what I did. I walked to the curb, stuck out my thumb, and waited for some kind stranger to pick me up. That day, I took a total of five rides from strangers. Every one of my drivers was pleasant and helpful. One older gentlemen lectured me all the while I was in his car on the dangers of hitchhiking.

I arrived at work before noon and regaled my co-workers with tales of my adventures on the road. The inventory came off without a hitch, and at the end of the night, a co-worker drove me half-way home, and my husband met me and brought me the rest of the way.

It took weeks, months even, for the city to recover from that incredible snowstorm. There was so much snow being cleared from the streets that the city workers had to haul it down to the lakefront and deposit it in mammoth piles that didn't melt until far into the spring. A favorite restaurant had a mini mountain of snow in the corner of its parking lot. They held a contest for the customers to see who could guess the day when it would finally melt away.

Ask any Chicagoan who was alive in January of 1967, and you will hear amazing stories of survival and strangers coming together to help one another in a time of difficulty. Some of these stories are frightening. Some of them are downright funny. But it's safe to say that everyone who was in Chicago in January of 1967 has a story to tell.

Photo by Enid Fefer

Belated Thank You Note

Carol Beu

To Ernie M, husband of my father's first cousin, Sigrid, born around 1895. As young men, Ernie and his brothers, George and Carl, enjoyed moderate success as a song-and-dance trio in Vaudeville. He later settled into an office job in the purchasing department at the American Can Company.

My memories of Ernie are of an older man, average height and weight, thinning grey hair, rumpled suit and a cigar constantly clenched between his teeth. His outgoing personality was always in evidence. In spite of his flamboyant ways, he was a beloved character in the family, and we knew that deep down he was a kind and caring person.

Dear Ernie,

I am writing this letter to say thank you for coming to my dance recital in 1948. I didn't understand it then, but in retrospect I realize that had to have been a mildly excruciating experience for you. All those giddy little girls—each one getting her moment in the spotlight—the program must have gone on for at least two hours. And you hung in there! At least, I think you did. Maybe you snuck out in the middle for a smoke. But that's okay. When the recital was over, you complimented me on my costume (fuchsia tutu, multi-color sparkled top, and toe shoes to match), and you told me that I danced very well. I doubt that was true—I've always been somewhat of a klutz. But in the end, what really mattered is that you showed up and you lied through your teeth. I really appreciate that.

Do you remember the wonderful family dinners we had over the years at our house on Fairfield Avenue or at your apartment in Andersonville? Those are some of my fondest memories. I remember that while the ladies were putting the finishing touches on the dinner, you, my dad, and your brothers would grab cocktails (Manhattans, I believe) and gather around the piano to harmonize. My dad played the piano while you and your brothers belted out the songs. Down by the Old Mill Stream seemed to be your favorite. If I close my eyes, I can still hear you all singing.

And remember the "Schweinhund Club"? At one of our dinners, somebody spilled something on the tablecloth. I believe it was your brother, George, who quipped, "Ah, you're a member of the Schweinhund Club!" (Leave it to one of the Maier boys to take one of the worst German insults ever—pig-dog!—and turn it into a club.) Everyone thought it was quite funny; and thereafter, any time one of us spilled something, we were initiated into the Schweinhund Club. As you probably recall, it didn't take long before every one of us was a member in good standing. (You can't take us anywhere, can you?) And then we were faced with the dilemma of what to do the next time someone made a mess at the table. The problem was solved when we decided that the most recent offender became the "Acting President of the Schweinhund Club." That title was passed from person to person until the day our wonderful dinners were no more.

And that reminds me....I have another thing to thank you for. Thanks so much for teaching me to play poker when I was in high school! It's a fun game and a valuable skill that served me well in later life. Now I know that we only played for pennies and that we didn't play serious poker. But I did love those screwball poker games (Night Baseball, Spit in the Ocean) that we all enjoyed after family dinners. And you taught me well. I will never forget the night that I faked you out with a rather mediocre hand and an excellent poker face. Oh, you were mad! The student had overtaken the teacher!! But I also like to think that you were a bit proud.

Wherever you are now, I hope that you think back on these happy memories and smile. I hope to see you again. Be ready to greet me with a Manhattan and a deck of cards with Down by the Old Mill Stream playing in the background.

Love,
Carol Ann

Photo by Robynne Wallace

Flamingo Hat

Carol Beu

My name is Fernando—Fernando Flamingo —Fernando Flamingo from Florida to be exact. I am the flamingo that you see on the hat on the front cover of this book. I bet you were surprised to see a flamingo sitting on hat. You are perhaps even asking yourself why a flamingo would be sitting on the top of a hat. Well, here's the story.

I was born on the coast of a small island in the Florida Keys. My early years were idyllic. I lived with my parents and my younger brother, Hernando. We were part of a large flock of flamingos and I was surrounded by family and friends. Our days were spent wading in the warm waters of a small bay and feasting on the glorious shrimp and algae that flourished there. We flamingoes get our bright pink color from the all the shrimp that we consume. I had quite an appetite and the result was that my feathers were very vivid—some even described them as "flagrantly flamingo".

As we were growing up, my brother and I amused ourselves frolicking and playing games like "Who can stand on one foot the longest?" or sometimes we would bump into one another trying to throw our opponent off balance and making him fall into the water. Sometimes we would fling shrimp at the back of the heads of the grownups. They would turn around in surprise and fury and try to see who had hit them. But Hernando and I would stand there on one foot acting like nothing had happened. It was fun and it was hilarious!

The elders warned us youngsters not to stray from the flock. They told us stories about places where the water was so cold that it became a solid that you could stand on. They said that we couldn't get food from this solid water and that we would starve to death— that is, if the blood in our bodies didn't turn solid first. A lot of my friends were very frightened by this story, but frankly, I thought it was just a bunch of flim-flam that they had made up to keep us close to the flock.

I've always been an adventurous kind of bird. I loved my home and family, but I would fantasize about one day leaving our quiet bay to see something of the world. I just knew there was something great, something exciting out there. I would watch the boats sailing back and forth out on the ocean. How I longed to join them. Everyday tourists came to look at our flock. They stood on the shore and took photos and admired us all. At the end of the day, they would get into their cars and leave. I wondered where they went and what it was like to be there. If only I could go and see for myself.

 A lot of people don't know this, but flamingoes can fly. I wanted to stretch my wings and fly away to discover a world I had never seen. But for some reason, I just couldn't take that first step to leave my home and family. And then one day, the decision was taken from me. On that day, there were a lot of tourists on the shore watching and admiring us. I was young, and I was proud. I had taken myself a little bit away from the flock so that the tourists could admire me alone. I stood there in the sunshine, balancing on one foot and I could almost hear them saying, "Isn't he magnificent?" I turned a bit so they could admire me in profile. And then it happened. One of the tourists came up behind me, threw a blanket over my head, and scooped me up. It all had happened so fast. The next thing I knew, I was thrown into their car and driven away from my beloved bay.

I don't know why, but for some reason, I wasn't frightened. To tell the truth, I was actually quite exhilarated by the whole thing. I sat there in the car and imagined the amazing sights that I would see. After a while, the car came to a stop and I was taken out and set down in front of a pleasant house. The people who had taken me smiled and brought me food and water. And so it was that I began my stay with the people I called "The Pleasant Family".

At first I really enjoyed my new home. The weather was warm. There was a small pond in the front yard, and I enjoyed standing in it. The food was different—not as tasty as the shrimp and algae that I was used to, but it was nourishing and I didn't mind.

And people would come by the house to marvel at me. You'd think they had never seen a flamingo before! People would walk by or slowly drive by just to get a glimpse of me. At first I was frightened and would freeze up every time I saw someone looking at me. It got so that people began to think that I was some kind of statue. I could hear them saying, "Oh! Isn't that lovely! We should get a flamingo statue for our yard too." And you know what? Pretty soon yards all over the area were sporting flamingo statues!

As I said, I was content--for a while. But then, my old wanderlust popped up again. I also saw that my new diet was taking its toll. Without a lot of shrimp to eat, my color was beginning to fade. No longer was I that vivid shade of pink. I was becoming a dusty grey bird. And so one day, when a junk truck was parked across the street, I took my chance. I strolled over to it and leaped into the back. I laid there as still as I could hoping that I would be mistaken for one of those flamingo yard statues. Eventually, the truck started and we headed off down the road. And I was once again off on a new adventure!

We drove around for hours, stopping here and there to pick up more junk that was then thrown into the back of the truck with me. Finally, we were no longer stopping and were on the open highway. The sun went down, and we continued on our way. Late at night, the truck slowed down and pulled into the parking lot of a large building. Overhead a bright neon sign flashed, "All You Can Eat Shrimp". I knew I had found my next home!

I spent the next few months living around the shrimp restaurant. During the day, I would stay hidden in the woods behind the building. Then late at night, I would sneak out and eat all of the leftover shrimp that had been thrown out during the day. Slowly my feathers began to show their vivid colors again and I was beginning to wonder where I should go next and how I could get there. It didn't take long before my questions were answered.

One afternoon, I was wandering through the woods and got a little too close to the edge. There happened to be a man standing behind the restaurant smoking a cigarette. I guess my vivid feathers stood out, and he spotted me. He came over with a big smile on his face. "Well, you're a beauty aren't you?" he said. "What are you doing here? This is no place for a flamingo!" And before I knew it, he threw his jacket around me and carried me out to his car.

It didn't take long to get to his home. He took me inside and I discovered that this man was an artist and I was going to live in an artist's studio. I must say, he knew a lot more about flamingoes than the Pleasant family. He fed me a proper diet of shrimp and algae so that I maintained my spectacular plumage. Soon I was his muse. He began to paint pictures of me. And then he began to sell them. They were so popular that my image was soon seen around the country on postcards, t-shirts, pot holders, shower curtains and many other items. Shops were filled with little statues of me, and tourists bought them to proudly display in their homes. My artist and I had become famous!

And then the most fantastic thing happened. SHE came into his studio. She was a princess from a country in far off Africa and oh, she was a magnificent woman! Her dress was made of a large, bright African print fabric. She stood tall and proud, and she had a way about her that commanded your attention. And she had a vision. She wanted to travel the world helping to spread peace and love. She knew that she needed to make just the right impression, and to do that she needed a flamboyant hat. She had been searching the world for such a hat, and one day she happened to read about my artist and me in a magazine. It was then that she knew. What she needed was a Flamingo Hat!

So right there in the studio, she made an offer to my artist, and I soon found myself being gently placed into her very luxurious car to start on the adventure of my life. After having had a very famous French milliner make a large hat in which I could sit, we began to travel the world. With me sitting serenely on her hat, she would proudly walk into palaces, capitols, and the homes of world leaders. What an entrance we made! People would gasp in surprise and admiration. Our picture was in newspapers and magazines everywhere. Everyone knew about us and wanted to meet us. We were celebrities!

Of course, nothing lasts forever and one day several years later, we had to face the fact I was getting too old for this kind of work. By this time, my princess had a whole flock of flamingoes at her palace, and I was replaced by a handsome young specimen who carried on the tradition of adorning the famous Flamingo Hat.

I then settled into a pleasant retirement at the palace. I even got married. Flora Flamingo from the Philippines and I were happily married for over 40 years. We had 4 children, Filbert, Phyllis, Philip, and Filomena.

Do I have any regrets? Am I sorry that I left Florida so many years ago? I must admit that often at night as I fall asleep my mind goes back to those frivolous days in my beloved bay with my family. But then I think of all the places I've been and all the things I've seen. And every summer my image appears on shirts and clothing around the world and thousands of little Fernando Flamingo souvenirs are found in homes everywhere. But most satisfying to me are the armies of flamingo statues that have graced front lawns for decades now. And to think that I, Fernando Flamingo from Florida, was the first! Frankly, I have to say, "No. No regrets." I remember once reading that creatures are as happy as they've made up their mind to be. I have to admit, I've been blessed, but I made up my mind long ago to be happy and I am.

Carol Beu, by her own admission, has not one poetic bone in her body. She had long been of the opinion that poetry is just an excuse to use fancy words. But her three years of exposure to the Budlong Woods Writers has caused her to change her mind, and she now delights in their poetic offerings. She has even made two forays into the world of poetry, relying heavily on group facilitator, Donna Pecore's, assertion that, "If you say it's a poem, it's a poem." Mostly, though, she confines her writings to memoirs and observations about the world around her.

Photo by Richard Kimball

A Rich Man

Daniel Cleary

I found a fresh minted penny
As bright as fabled gold
Upon the pavement where it shone
A fine thing to behold

As if the sun, by some mischance
Had fallen from the sky
Momentarily at my feet
& there had caught my eye

I quickly swooped & picked it up
Feeling a gust of grace
As if the entire world I knew
Had suddenly given place

To a whole new way of thinking,
Of feeling, if you will—
There in the space of one short breath
I felt my being fill

"I am a rich man," I intoned
Regardless of who heard
& took off briskly from that spot
Without another word

Photo by Donna Pecore

Poem for (MCW)

Daniel Cleary

She comes bearing a poem in tow
A batch of stanzas in her wake
A wealth of words that I may know
In time the proper path to take
When I set out in retrospect
Her wayward motion to inspect.

It's all there from the very start
Before I even know for sure
Just what it is that stirs my heart
& makes it prey to her allure.
It's in plain view yet hid from sight
A kind of secretive delight.

It's simply part of who she is
Implicit in the way she walks
Or moves about in random bliss
Or blithely gushes when she talks
To whomsoever stands nearby
Or manages to catch her eye.

It's in her laissez-faire, her poise
The way she cuts & wears her hair
Her encompassing gaze, her eyes
& how she glances everywhere—
Her small nose slightly retroussé
That I could talk about all day.

She'll take it with her when she goes
Leaving me for a while bereft
Up gathered in the furbelows
The carefree flounces of her skirt
Departing through an open door
Perhaps new regions to explore.

She'll take it with her, leaving me
To make the best of what I have
Remembering the poetry
The inspiration that she gave.
If she returns I'll share with her
The small poem I have written here.

Friends

Daniel Cleary

We name those friends whose steady charge
Throughout our lives has been to show
A mixed relation by & large
To what we care about & know.
Bypassing all our many flaws
They gravitate within our sphere
Devoid of any false applause
They know exactly who we are.

If what I say above is true
The opposite must be the same
We become friends with others who
In spite of turmoil play the game.
They make the best of what they've got
As with a fiddle stick & strings
Being happy when the world is not
They rise above on paper wings.

But friends are sometimes those who pass
Like silent shadows in the night
Who first come close & then, alas
Without much fanfare fade from sight.
We think of them from time to time
Keeping in mind their lively charms
Say each of them aloud by name
Who came & went between our arms.

Friends in the long run are what we
Increasingly rely upon
As days get tougher & we see
Old friends departing, one by one.
We hope to gather as we go
New friends, perhaps, as fashions change
& we, in turn, expand & grow
& life seeks out a further range.

We hope to gather if we can,
& if the world approve us still
New friends; in time increase our span
Of friendship, laughter & goodwill.
Though life draws grimly to a close
We hope to find these last few days
Some small contentment & repose
With friends yet while the music plays.

Wake Up Call

Daniel Cleary

Where's the music that might wake us
From our unfathomed sleep
Might resurrect and wholly break us
So we begin to weep?

Where are the precepts, plain and simple
Posted beyond our ken
As if in some forgotten temple
Where pilgrims say amen

That would with inspiration find us
Enlighten us to boot
And hopefully at last remind us
Of what was once the truth?

Where, in the end, is our compunction
At what we have become
Heeding at last the fierce injunction
Of what needs to be done?

In feathered sleep time rocks the baby
Thoughtfully to and fro
Someday, perhaps, tomorrow, maybe
When it's too late, we'll know.

Photo by Carol Beu

Gratitude

Daniel Cleary

In gratitude for the good day
The small birds swoop and dive
Engaged in what seems random play
Happy to be alive.

Observing them, inversely, I
Share in their gratitude
Their tumbling anthem to the sky
And, looking up, thank God.

Having come a long way, from Tipperary town in Ireland that is, a long time ago, **Daniel Cleary** endeavors, with the aid of meter and rhyme, to transmit delicate states of poetic feeling for those with the nerve to pay him heed. Daniel has three books that can be found by googling his name. They are A Few Stray Leaves (Lagoons Editions, 2015), Elegy for James Gerard and Other Poems for the Larger Voice (Fractal Edge Press, 2004), and The Green Ribbon (Enright House of Ireland, 1993).

Photo by Enid Fefer

Barn Dance

Enid Fefer

Only thing on a Saturday night
Spin your gal to the left, then right
And make sure to hold on tight.

Louise and Ike, old-timers
Dance with each other
As if they had been close
Hugging around a camp fire

Old Ike, a barrel chest, as an ancient washing machine
He could wring your heart with a hearty crank
Perhaps dry your tears
Heavy-footed like an old tar road
Melting in the summer breeze

Louise took a liking to old Ike
He was broken-in
As if old steady furniture in a holiday cabin
A little lived-in is nice, she thought

She's mighty fine, he thought.
Hair blowing like laundry over a vegetable garden
I'll bet she smells like cucumbers

Her smile, open like a screened porch letting in the breeze
But keeping out those thief flies
He could see her heart, he felt that
Open but staying safe
Gentle attraction at the barn dance

Photo by Donna Pecore

Imagine a River

Enid Fefer

A holy river with gods and pagodas sliding down past the sloping hills and the straw cottages. The workers must live and raise their children here.

Satong. Second born in her poor family, she wishes to go to school. Boys may attend but only after the rice harvest has been completed.

Satong, a sweet child with long dark hair and pale white skin. She loves the wild flowers that grow along the river banks and kiss fragrant air.

Hasing, her older brother, has learned to read a little, but he is silent with his sister. Big and boastful with his quill and ink, he makes shaky letters on rice paper.

Satong, lovely, yet with willful wishes, not desirable in a girl in the low country where the river runs, she is petite and agile; she likes to dance among flowers.

She dances as the river flows. Pretends to be the river, with its rocks and currents and snaking directions. Swish, swish, swish.

She whispers and turns around and around until dizzy and falls into delicate wild flowers and tall grass.

She would love to go to school; women shall never be allowed to do such a thing. She would like to sing and write her soul on rice paper, but that is not allowed.

She must be obedient. It is the way of the valley, the way of the river and the way of lucky families who have good fortune.

Beautiful orange, red and yellow butterfly lands on her delicate arm; she is entranced. She bends to kiss it.

Just then Hasing throws his weather-tattered straw hat, which flies over her arm, and the beautiful creature flies away; leaves her in a sad and bitter moment.

Her butterfly was the only soft connection she has made since the sun came up in the sky two hours ago.

Angus McGee

Enid Fefer

His name was Angus McGee, but sadly, I never met my grandfather, even though I was named after him. My dad is Angus Jr., and I am Angus III. I have heard many tales about him, and I wish I had been born earlier so I could have met him. I was too young to remember Riverview, but that was one of the places where he had a brilliant but tainted career. He grew up on the south side and went into the Navy. He went in young because there weren't many jobs during the Depression and too many mouths to feed at home. When he finished his tour of duty, he came back to Chicago and tried work at the steel mills in Indiana, but that didn't last long enough for a second paycheck. My dad told me he had a penchant for drink, fighting, and of course, the ladies. I heard a story that he got into a fight with another man and sent the other guy to the plant nurse for stitches. His pictures show him strong and handsome with a flare for the dramatic. He tried selling used automobiles, but he would get into arguments with customers, hence not enough of a paycheck.

He tried a few other jobs: Fuller Brush salesman, ice cream bicycle route, even a job selling hot dogs at the ball park for the White Sox. But he hit his stride when a friend from the neighborhood told him about Riverview. The owners loved him at first sight, as my dad tells it. They told him he could be the Strong Man who could "talk to the dead." He hadn't met my grandma yet, so he had asked his best gal, Bitsy, to make him a costume: really short striped fighter pants and a silky lined robe for ringside warm up. He bought some stage makeup at a store in a south side Jewish neighborhood near the Yiddish theater.

The Riverview guys sent him to a prop shop on the premises where they made him a pair of wings. I guess they wanted to make him look like he could fly with the angels, speak to the dead, and bring back messages to the "suckers" who paid him a few bucks just to talk to their departed love ones or maybe to deliver an angry message to cheaters and thieves.

Angus had a great little stage; they built heavy medallions to recreate the look of a champion belt for winning a big fight. I saw a picture of him, and he was quite handsome. The men liked him because they thought they could be like him, but the women, they would discreetly wink at Angus McGee. You see, they were there with their husbands or boyfriends. Women did not go to Riverview unaccompanied back then—too much riffraff. Women never went there alone.

My grandpa Angus was not a great speaker. With little education, he was more a man of action than of words. But that worked out fine for him. He would stand there in an iron-front-stare, deep in concentration. He would read a small book or from some pamphlet occasionally, making deliberately vague quotes, and many in the audience would think the words were directed at them personally.

This was Angus McGee's longest job, my father tells me. He liked working there, and he liked the companionship: the bearded lady (which was an effeminate man,) the snake eater, the fire eater, and the two-headed goat with his trainer. Don't ask me about that. I don't know, and neither did my dad.

Well, Angus eventually married my grandma Gert, and they had three boys. My dad was the youngest. Angus lasted a long time there, until there was a raid and he and others were arrested for some scheme to defraud the Riverview family. He did a small stint at Cook County Jail, but they couldn't make the charges stick. Angus had to go back to car sales, but he became a little less combative and he did all right after that. But he always missed Riverview. He was a star there.

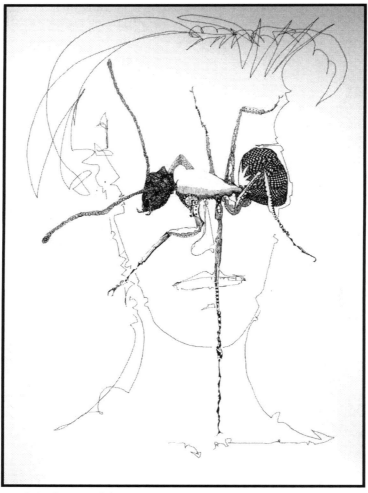

Original Artwork by Tony Pigott

Dear Victoria

Enid Fefer

Dear Victoria:

I am doing well. The doctors say I am improving, but they will not tell me that I can return home. Please tell Papa and Mama that I am handling myself well and that I have not set any fires since I arrived. They do room checks here, and they have taken away my sealing wax and matchsticks and tell me that I must try to involve myself in womanly and genteel activities. I have never liked embroidery, but they claim it will clam my nerves.

We have tea at 3:00 pm, and most of the other "guests" do not hold interesting or valuable insights into the new century. Many women blather and squawk about their spouses and how they have been cheated out of their dowries or that their husband's mistresses take too much of their men's slender earnings.

They do let us sketch the hills and the pond with its sea grass and silly geese. The geese are maddening and tortuous, and since they are in mating season, well, they just make such a racket. I enjoy the painting and sketching, and I am becoming much better with my brushes.

There is an irritating man here by the name of François. Victoria, the rumor is that he poisoned the family goat. To think of it, killing an innocent like that. He has told me that he adores fiery sunsets, and that has made my heart go aflutter.

I am not truly sure why I like fire so much. It is so lovely in its autumnal colors, and it dances with the wind or even the slightest movement in the air. Even a tiny wash of hand can dance the wick and flame.

They are summoning us for the evening repast, so I must take my leave and I will write again soon.

Yours,
Emily

Dear Victoria:

You must set the alarm and get Mama and Papa to secure my release.

I am so deadly bored here. I don't like talking to the Doctor Elliswich. He continues to probe my relationship with Mama and especially Papa. He is most annoying and seems to look down upon me. I so desire some excitement. The sketching and occasional watercolor do not maintain my interest. François has taken an interest in me, I do fear. He also pays quite a bit of attention to the geese.

Last night, Francois gave me a matchstick that Mr. Grice, the butler and serving steward, mistakenly dropped while lighting all the many candles at our delicate dinning table. I hugged it to my bosom. I slept with that matchstick under my pillow for three nights. I do believe that François has taken a liking to me, but I am not sure he is a suitable match for me.

Yours,
Emily

Dear Victoria:

I must tell you that there is a big mystery here. Five of the geese at the pond have been found expired. It is so sad, but it is much more quiet here. I just can't bear to think that dear François is responsible. Where could he have secured any poison? No one has accused him of anything.

Yours,
Emily

Dear Victoria:

I am sure that you have been contacted by the sheriff or the constable by now. Yes, It is true. I am the guilty one. The sleeping wing of the women's quarter has burnt to the ground. The fire was most beautiful. The waves of red, orange, and yellow roared like a massive beast and lit up the night sky. Tiny licks of red of orange jumped and circled the air as the flames devoured the wooden building. It was glorious.

So, I will never see you or our parents again. Franç+ois and Dr. Elliswich were brought down by the fire and have left their earthly home. The matron of the laundry was also killed. It was not my desire to see anyone perish, but I must tell you the fire was the most spectacular feast of the senses that I have ever witnessed in my life. Yes, my life will end soon. The constable has told me that I shall be hanged in a fortnight. Dearest Victoria, do not be sad. I shall depart with no regrets. Perhaps I will miss the loud geese.

Yours,
Emily

Alfie Monroe

Enid Fefer

Alfie is my best friend and has been since the first grade. We are now in fifth grade, and we both think President Eisenhower is the best ever. My name is Billy, and I am the leader/captain of the green monkeys. I am searching for Alfie right now, but it is mid-day and Alfie is rather good at being stealthy. I hear his mom call him from the front porch for some lemonade, but Alfie is really stubborn and won't let himself be captured by me. The cold lemonade doesn't even bring him out. I can remember the last time we were swimming at Pete's pond having inner tube races. He went over turtle, under the inner tube, but he would not let go of the tube and almost drown. I can see him now, oceans of water streaming from his bluish lips, an unstoppable expelling of damp air in the form of gagging and pumping lungs. But it was in our rules not to let go of the tube. Alfie was stubborn like me. We both liked to win.

I hear his ma call us again for some lemonade. I began crouching along the side path between our houses. I think Alfie might be in back of the tin shed, the one where the bicycles, the lawnmower, and 20 pounds of green garden hose are stored. I have my Uzi strapped back on my shoulder, and I come along the side of the tin shed. We named this Station Moropo. I look behind the shed but no Alfie.

"Alfie Monroe, you better come an' answer me if you know what's good for you!" Alfie's mother is getting mad. I can see her standing on their large wrap-around porch. With a little bit of wind, the porch swing is creaking. "Alfie. ANSWER me!"

But Alfie is not the type to surrender. Neither am I. I put a stern and steady hand on my Mattel Uzi 9055, push my cap back on my sweaty forehead and crawl, low to the ground, to the other side of Station Moropo. I can hear him breathing rather heavily. I know I have him now. I reach for my Uzi and disengage it from my shoulder. On my belly, I come around the next corner pointing my 9055. Instead, I find Winky, the Monroes' mutt. He looks startled and runs for cover under the front porch. Winky pushes his scrawny body through the two broken lattice panels underneath the wrap-around porch. Alfie and I would laugh about the dark and damp soil underneath the porch, saying it would be a great place to hide evidence. We had a theory that Mr. Carson, our teacher, had been buried there, but he returned from a three-week absence, explaining that there had been a death in his family.

Mr. Carson looked all fat and old to us; a big jowly face with creases and small eyes, a fat neck with sucked down his head into his stocky body. When he was concentrating, you could see his little glass gold frames get cloudy with body mist. I hear my ma talking to Alfie's ma. "It's a shame that Alice left him. Now he will have to take care of himself. He looks so lost. Poor man."

I am determined to capture Alfie today. Alfie is very smart. Yes, he is good with reading and sums, but then he always gets into some kind of trouble. Not bad trouble, but trouble nonetheless. Telling jokes and fooling around. I can't remember any jokes right now, but he was good at telling them. I guess I am as stubborn as Alfie, but I don't get into trouble like him.

Alfie was the one to argue with Reverend Telken about angels being more powerful than God. Alfie liked the idea that angels could fly around and see things from up above and help people or play little tricks on them but that God was old and kind of had to stay in one place. Reverend Telken didn't take kindly to that kind of talk, but Alfie had a way with logic and I liked his ideas.

He also had upset Mr. Carson. During math, Alfie told the kids in our class that one was not a real number because one times one is only one. He had us believing that the number one was a big mistake. He persuaded the Hillburn twins to go to the back of the math books and change some of the answers down by one, just to eradicate the number one. Mr. Carson just sputtered and told Alfie to go to Mr. Pearson's office when he found out about the math mutiny against the number one. Going to Mr. Pearson was no real punishment. I had only been there one time. We played with the toys on his desk. Mr. Pearson seemed cautious. Maybe he was concerned that his secretary would come in and take his toys away and tell him to get back to work. So he told us to close the door so we could play with the toys.

I am starting to think that lemonade would be real nice, but Mrs. Monroe had disappeared into the house. Alfie is hiding pretty good, so I decide to go ask Mrs. Monroe for some refreshments on my own. I open the screen door. We never knock in the summer since it's just the screen door. Winky can get out on his own, but when he wants to come in he whines and scratches until someone opens the door for him. Winky was useful when we could capture him. He was often a prisoner of war. He had a large steel crate and after negotiation for an exchange of prisoners, Winky would yelp and whine, then we would let him out. Dirt would fly off of his hind legs as he dove under the porch.

I go into the front parlor. An old worn, yellowed old piano is right by the bay window. The piano is squarish and squat with some straight line carvings above the keys. It's an old used piano from Mrs. Monroe's parents. I heard that Mrs. Monroe's parents became sorry that they gave that old piano to their daughter and her new husband, especially since they soon suspected that Mr. Monroe beat on Mrs. Monroe. She never played that piano.

Alfie had shown me the back of the piano one time when his parents were not around. He had scratched some secret code there and slid the piano up against the wall to protect the code being discovered. I have a desire to go over and touch the keys and look behind the old thing to look at Alfie's codes, but I think I will say hello to Alfie's ma before I go messing with her belongings. Mrs. Monroe hands me a glass of lemonade, which I drink fast. It is gone, and she hands me another. She opens the window over her kitchen sink and continues with her kitchen work.

I go back out on the wrap-around porch and sit on the old swing. I call out, "OK Alfie, I concede. Come out and I will discuss the conditions of surrender."

40

Yet Alfie is quiet. The rules are that you must sign a surrender declaration and settle up the casualties of war. I jump down off the porch and go sit on the empty tree stump in the yard. Then I see Alfie coming towards me. "Shall we settle up, General?" I ask him.

He is not talking, and he looks weird. He takes a letter out of his back pocket. It has been folded and refolded many times. Alfie looks old and tired for a boy our age. He says "I found this yesterday in my Ma's pantry while looking for provisions for our campaign." He explains that he has read it over many times but never could believe it.

I tell him, "I don't want to read it." I am worried.

Alfie says "It is from my Pa. He is going to leave my Ma." We both sit on the old gnarled stump of the tree. The game is over, and so is Alfie's childhood.

Enid Fefer tells us, "I've been thinking about writing my whole life. I just rarely did it." After almost 40 years as a psychotherapist, adjunct faculty member, clinical supervisor, and consultant, Enid has retired and now has more time to write fiction and personal narrative, enjoy photography, and make art.

Photo by Carol Beu

The Stuff I See

Ann Fiegen

My adult children have often expressed their frustration in navigating what they view as my obsession with stuff. Walls too burdened with photographs and water-colors, surfaces too cluttered with objects, cabinets overloaded with china and glass-ware, a garden too frequently punctuated by rusting wrought iron and stone...they find it overwhelming, and I get it. I am not immune to the fact that there is a charm connected with less is more. I am not beyond coveting an uncluttered surface. And yet, I consistently wage battle between my wants and needs in the stuff department. The battle centers around the fact that I am a compulsively clean hoarder. Just think about that for a moment...consider the internal war of one who loves her stuff yet needs for her surroundings to be dust free and orderly. Now that's conflict!

The OCD clean me, particularly around Christmas when the decorations take over the house, sometimes thinks about scaling down, putting stuff away in boxes, reducing the numbers of paintings on the walls and objects on surfaces and selling my excesses on eBay. Occasionally, I give it a shot. I start with the walls. Which paintings should I box up? Some of the vintage watercolors garnered from antiqu-ing excursions across the country? No, they make me happy and remind me of time spent with a good friend seeking treasures in dusty shops in small towns far and wide. They connect me to the long-dead artists who created them and put them in those lovely old frames, artists who would most certainly love that, after all these years, they are on display rather than boxed up in someone's basement, or worse yet, destroyed. No, the paintings have to stay.

How about the photographs? There are way too many of those. Can I box up the pic-tures of my boys when they were boys, with their freckled faces, bad haircuts, and toothless grins, the camera-captured innocence that abounds, their little boy selves that still lie within the men they have become? Of course not.

OK, not those, but how about the ancient family pictures, those fading black and whites of long-gone souls with whom I share DNA? Boxing them up would provide a blank wall and several unadorned dressers and table tops. And so I try. The first one I take down is of my father's family, ten Irish children posed in their Sunday best and looking directly at the camera. My father, the youngest, and his next oldest brother stand in front because they are the smallest. They are wearing ties that are too big, and their shirts have come untucked. Their older siblings surround them, all looking somewhat alike and very serious. The picture captures them together and holds them there. When I see it, I share that moment. How can I possibly let them go? Put them in a box? I don't think so. They stay where they are.

With walls intact, I move to surfaces. For sure I can get rid of some of this stuff. How about the whimsical Leprechauns from a charming shop in Kinsale, bought on that rainy day of shopping and pub comfort food? Or the carved walrus from Alaska, an unexpected gift from a man I loved to mark our spectacular trip there? The little Hummel from Bavaria? The enchanting girl from Prague? Hand-sculpted creations gifted me by my boys when they were small? One by one I consider each piece on the surfaces in my home and come to the same conclusion. They are there because they mark the times of my life that should not be forgotten. To remove them is like removing those moments from my life, and why would I ever want to do that?

And so, time after time, my hoarder self wins the battle, and I continue to live with too much clutter to satisfy the cleanliness freak that shares her soul space. My stuff remains in place, in every nook and cranny of my house, on every wall, on every flat surface...the stuff that makes me smile, sometimes cry, but always reminds me of my wonderful life and of the village that has helped make it so. Too much? Perhaps, but everything in my house speaks to the gifts I have been given, the gifts of a rich, full life and glorious friends and family with whom to share it.

I could choose to box it all up and declutter. I could take the things I love and pack them away in the garage or basement. I could live out the rest of my life in neat and orderly surroundings with clear walls and clutter-free surfaces, ultimately leaving little to do for my children when I depart. Of course I could, but...

What if when I could no longer see my stuff, I forgot all the reasons I chose to have it on display?

What if my being able to see it all is key to my remembering all the life gifts that I have been given?

What if in its absence I forgot, even for a moment, that life is an adventure, friendships are treasures, and love abounds?

About that clutter? It's just fine. Perfect even.

Photo by Tom Stark

That's All Folks

Ann Fiegen

Earlier this summer, I noticed this perfect little hole on the outside of my house. You know, the kind of hole used by Jerry in the cartoon series he did with Tom... that perfectly rounded entrance to his mouse domicile through which he always scampered just in the nick of time when Tom was in hot pursuit. For a while I ignored it, but on the day I witnessed the tail end of a furry critter running in, I thought perhaps I shouldn't ignore it anymore. My first call was to an exterminator.

"Mice," I told him, "I have mice in residence under my porch."

"I'm in the neighborhood," said he. "I can be there within the hour."

He arrived as promised, and I tried to ignore the image in my head of Jerry scurrying around his little pied-à-terre looking for a hiding place to avoid a certain death at the hands of a man whose truck boasted TERMINIX RODENT CONTROL on its side panel. Even I was a little scared of the Terminix guy. He came bearing instruments of rodent destruction, and with Jerry's frantic image in my head, I pointed out the hole and quickly left the scene so as not to witness the process. In short order, Mr. Terminix opened my door a crack and announced that mice were not my problem, but rather chipmunks.

Now, because of my past association with Jerry, I knew pretty much about mice, but other than the fact that I liked their Christmas music, I knew nothing about chipmunks.

"What do we do?" I asked.

He responded that we didn't do anything because chipmunks were not on the list of rodents that could be exterminated. Instead I would have to contact a wildlife specialist. The only good news from the exterminator was that he would only charge me $50 instead of the usual $100 for an initial visit. So I wrote the check for $50, kind of a steep price I thought for only the knowledge that my rodent in residence did not look like Jerry, but more like either Alvin, Simon, or Theodore.

Apparently, there are a number of wildlife experts in the area. I chose ABC HUMANE WILDLIFE CONTROL and made an appointment. Bright and early the next morning I was greeted by a man wearing a hat with fir trees and bears on it, a camo shirt, sunglasses, camp shorts, knee socks, and hiking boots (de rigueur I guess for wildlife experts). Again, I directed him to the hole while having a new mental image, this time of Alvin rather than Jerry not being fooled for a moment by the word HUMANE on the side of the truck, and frantically running for cover.

Camo man quickly evaluated the situation and called me out to define my role in the process. There were cages strategically placed on my property and baited with peanut butter to tempt the prey. He told me to check the cages frequently and gave me a number to call when there was a score to request pick up of the captured prey for removal and placement in someone else's neighborhood several miles away. I was somewhat skeptical but wrote him a check for the $125. initial fee anyway. As I watched him leave, I had a sinking feeling. It was just me and five peanut butter–laden cages against the world of wildlife, and I wasn't sure I would emerge victorious.

The day went by. I checked the cages regularly, but they remained hopelessly empty. Just before I went to bed, I went outside in pajamas carrying a flashlight for one final check. Front yard, clear. As I headed to the back I heard the sound of something thrashing around in one of the cages. Sounds a little big for a chipmunk, I thought. I shined the light in the cage and staring back at me was a baby squirrel with terror in his eyes. Instead of Alvin, or Simon, or Theodore, Rocky began hurling himself around the cage and making pathetic little squirrel squeals that told me I couldn't just leave him there until the next day for release. And so, I put on a pair of rubber gloves, held my breath, and cautiously opened the cage. He bolted out. At that moment I knew how the kid felt in Free Willie when he watched Willie bound through the ocean's waves to freedom.

Day two of the hunt produced two chipmunks who remained relatively calm in their cages, nibbling at the peanut butter until a different man in a camo shirt, sunglasses, but no hat, knee socks, or boots came and picked them up. I must admit they were cute little buggers, as were the four others who met the same fate in the two days that followed. Each time, after writing a check for $50, I watched the captured critters be loaded into a van and driven off into the sunset.

By the end of the week it was over. The cages had remained empty for two days, and camo man and I agreed that it was safe to cease the hunt. He gathered up his cages and left. One week, five service calls, and $325 later, the critters were gone and all that remained was the hole in my house and one, lonely, forgotten trap in my bushes.

This morning, while sitting in the yard, I saw him right there next to the pot of begonias. He moved away fast, but he didn't fool me for a second. I recognized him right away...two little beady eyes, stripes down his back, mouse-like tail...I know a chipmunk when I see one. This time, however, remembering the total dollars spent on the last humane removal process, I have a better plan. Let's see...Forgotten cage, check. Peanut butter, check. Rubber gloves, check, and I know I have a camo shirt someplace.

Forever Aftering

Ann Fiegen

On that Thursday morning, as on most Thursday mornings, I was in my kitchen watering the plants. That room, bathed in morning sunlight, was my sacred space. It hosted a variety of growing things, all of which I tended to religiously, loving the fact that I was able to keep them flourishing. The most spectacular plant in the room was a Boston fern whose bright green fronds spanned the entire width of the window above which it hung. I often spoke to that plant, misted it regularly, and dosed it with plant food whenever its green became a little less vibrant. It was perfection, and I took great pride in my nurturing skills.

The radio was on, and as I poured the plant a soaking drink, a German psychologist known as Dr. Ruth was taking calls from listeners who had questions about their sex lives. Small but mighty, what she lacked in stature, Dr. Ruth made up for in chutzpah. At a time when it was not a matter for public discussion, she spoke openly about human sexuality. No topic was too indelicate; no question was left unanswered.

There were a couple of callers asking the usual questions involving premature ejaculation, impotence, and female orgasm, and then came a call from a listener who suspected her husband might be gay. She sounded nervous and more than a little embarrassed to ask the question, but Dr. Ruth didn't miss a beat. With her characteristic accent, she replied..."My dahlink, ven you even sink your husband is gay, he is gay." And with that simple exchange, the question that had owned the back of my mind for so long was answered, and I knew my life would never be the same.

It was a freeze-frame moment for me. Everything around me stopped, and I stood, watering can in hand amid all my green perfection, staring out the window.

What the hell do I do now?

During the weeks that followed, I vacillated between not eating and being unable to stop, sleeping all the time and not sleeping at all, racing through days like a whirling dervish and vegging mindlessly on the couch. I bottomed out in September. The kids were back in school, and I still had more questions than answers. Abjectly paralyzed, I simply went to bed and there I stayed, in my place of sanctuary, where I wasn't afraid, where nothing had to change. Outside the sanctuary was confusion, hard decisions, and a life so altered that I had no idea how to live it. And so, in bed I remained, calmed by the sameness and predictability of each day. My husband filled in the empty spaces as best he could, silently hoping that the next day would be different.

Friends, family, and co-workers began to worry about me. Sometimes I'd take their calls and go on about my mystery virus and its debilitating effects on my energy level. I told the same story at work and tapped into my unused sick days. My kids came in periodically, lingering only as long as it took to provide CliffsNotes versions of their days, and then leaving to resume their places in the comfort zone of the life that was going on outside my four walls. I don't know how many days went by. Five? A week?

Finally there came the morning that I began to fear that my retreat from life would jeopardize my being a fit mother. And so, I rose from my self-imposed coma and resumed my place among the living. My mantra became one goal a day, and I pretty much stuck to it, constantly moving towards shaping a new reality, one in which our broken family could regroup with the least amount of trauma and emotional pain.

In 1981 gay was something Rock Hudson was still pretending not to be, and coming out was what young society debutantes did in white dresses at cotillions. My mother thought Liberace was sexy for God's sake. My hairstylist was gay, as was the bartender at the private club where I worked, but my husband? Whose husband was gay? No one I had even heard of, but the truth was that while I had been married to my first love for 17 years, it was all irreparably wrong because I was a woman and he was a gay man. My husband was gay, the ultimate irreconcilable difference. And so, I filed for divorce, and we moved forward because there was nothing else to do, no other choice that could be made.

Divorce was a grueling process. There were lawyers, custody arrangements, financial decisions, all of which required answers before the court date that loomed in our future. Times were different then, and for my strictly Catholic born-and-bred husband to admit that he was gay to anyone, even himself, was impossible. I was convinced our then teenaged sons needed to be protected from a truth that might be damaging to their relationship with their father and add confusion to their own emerging sexualities. I was not interested in outing him. The charade needed to be maintained in order for us all to emerge less scarred. And so, we moved through divorce proceedings with neither of us ever even whispering to anyone the truth that had shattered life as we knew it.

It was a painful journey. There was anger, hurt, and great sadness. We wrestled with constructing the best new reality for our sons, eventually working out a shared custody agreement where he and I moved in and out of our home and an apartment we shared at six-month intervals. This allowed our boys' lives to remain relatively constant and provided us both with a continuing live-in relationship for half of each year. With sheer determination we maintained our arrangement for six years until our youngest son was out of high school, at which point my husband and I each took a deep breath and moved toward yet another new reality, one in which our contact with one another was minimal, polite if not gracious.

Disconnects have always been ridiculously hard for me. I tend to attach and hang on for dear life, and my connection with my former husband was no exception to that tendency. The experiences we had shared were life defining, and the conjoined hopes and dreams of our very young selves bound us with ties that were not easy to sever. Eventually, however, with time, the great healer, we were able to move on, and there were many years when we had no contact at all aside from events related to our children and eventually to our grandchildren.

Even time, however, could not erase all that we had once shared: his working three jobs to keep us afloat on a teacher's salary for those few years when I needed to stay at home with babies; the boys' birthday parties, sporting events, pinewood derbies, and Halloween costumes; the sleepless nights holding feverish bodies or comforting after bad dreams; that time of dancing together smoothly and easily in step and in tune to the music of life as a family.

Several years ago my former husband and I were seated next to one another at our grandbaby's birthday party, and we began to reconnect. For the first time since our divorce, our conversation wasn't strained. Perhaps the wine helped, but when he made me laugh, I remembered how funny he was. During our discussion of a book we had both recently read, I remembered how smart he was. The commonality that had once brought us together was working again, and we settled into a comfortable place that we both enjoyed. Why wouldn't we? We were still the same people who had once promised to love one another forever. And so, in the months that followed, we tested the waters of yet another reality. We became friends.

Now we're in a place where we do together the things that old friends do. We go to the movies, see a play, call and text one another to share a laugh or concern. We meet friends for lunch or dinner and discuss old times, current events, the beauty and brilliance of our grandchildren, and the hilarious/tragic issues of these, our "Golden Years."

Strange but kind of nice, really, to be actively involved with this man with whom I spent so much of my past. Yes, in a way I am kind of dating my former husband who happens to be gay, but times have changed. We have changed. Thankfully, maturity has given us the wisdom to know how important it is to nurture all connections of the heart like Boston ferns, allowing them to flourish rather than destroying them with anger and resentment...to know that love does indeed endure if we allow for its own form of limited perfection.

Life is so full of surprises, bends in the road, unanticipated outcomes that catch all of us off guard and open doors we thought were shut forever. Thankfully I have never totally abandoned my belief in fairy tales. And now I bask in the knowledge that in life, as in every fairy tale, there is always the possibility of a happy ending and that these happy endings are as diverse as the tales they close. After so many decades of believing that my forever after had been denied, I now know for sure that I was wrong. On the contrary, it was granted. Forever afters just don't always look the same.

At the End of the Hall

Ann Fiegen

In a private room at the end of the hall, my beautiful friend lay dying. Just hours before, she had said she would see me in the morning. I counted on that, but when I returned her, eyes were closed. During the night, while I was sleeping, or perhaps while I was awake and thinking about her, she let go of consciousness and began to take her leave. She was now somewhere else, at some amorphous place halfway between life and death, where she just couldn't see me at all.

We were all there, the people who loved her, and as the morning passed, we each took time to whisper our tearful goodbyes. Her boys were losing their mother; her husband, his wife; her siblings, their sister; and I, my lifelong friend, all losses unimaginable as we listened to her breathe, here with us yet far away. The music of her favorite ballet, Swan Lake, played softly, and the sound of her breathing became tied to the music, creating a kind of serenity in that room at the end of the hall. We spoke quietly and cried silently so as to maintain the peace that was there, the peace that should accompany the dying process. We knew that if, in that place somewhere between life and death, she could hear that elegant score, she was smiling, perhaps even dancing.

There came a time when her brother and I sat down on either side of her, listening to her breathe. He took her left hand, I her right, and there we remained with her between us. We spoke quietly about how funny she was, and how strong, how smart she was and how brave, how stubborn she was and how kind. How she could dance, and cook, and entertain like no other. How great she was as lawyer, mother, sister, and friend. We spoke of her ability to always select the perfect gift for every occasion and wrap it in beautiful paper with handmade bows. Her gifts surround me: the cat weathervane poised to leap at any moment from my garage roof, the hand-painted punch set, the heart-shaped earrings, the vintage liqueur carafes painted with winter scenes are all among her perfect gifts that I treasure.

As we spoke, I hoped she could hear us. I hoped she could hear our words spoken while holding her hands as she lay dying in that room at the end of the hall, and in hearing us know how much she was loved.

And then, after what seemed like a long time, there came the instant when I felt her leave. She simply shifted from here to there, and I felt it. I spoke her brother's name, and we both held our breath waiting for another of hers. There was none, leaving music of Swan Lake the only sound in the room. She was gone, taking with her huge chunks of our hearts and leaving an empty spot in our lives. We who had for so long delighted in her presence, now, like the strains of Swan Lake, had to go on without her.

Her final gift, the unique privilege of holding her hand when she took her leave, was her most perfect gift to me. Wrapped in love rather than beautiful paper and handmade bows, this gift outshone all that came before. It was precious, and priceless, and uniquely personal. It closed the final chapter of our story with a gift surpassing all others, the gift of a perfect ending.

Ann Fiegen has come home again to her city roots by becoming a part of the Budlong Woods Writers. Happily retired, she now enjoys time sufficient to do the things she loves. She shares precious hours with her six grandchildren, spends lazy summer days hanging out in her garden, travels, joins often with the ladies who lunch, and finally, she writes...about what she has learned, loved and lived through.

Photo by Enid Fefer

The Cause of Crows

Gay Guard-Chamberlin

Hey

           hey

                hey you

                        down there.

I'm talking to you.

Listen now. I can tell you about finding things. Me?

                                    I'm an expert.

My kind are jacks-of-all-trades   the collectors & cataloguers
                      clever curators of clutter.
           We're the ones who invented the knickknack shelf.

Here's what I have so far:
1 brass hinge / 1 plastic soldier missing head / 8 acorns /
4 really good twigs / 3 earrings (1 red, 1 turquoise, 1 clear as water) /
1 crab claw / 1 dime / 2 nails plus rust / 1 mouse skull / 1 green button
with dangling black thread / 2 more good twigs

So how about you?   What have you found today?

Hey

                hey HEY!

Stupid wingless two-legs

don't you see

this whole world

is shining?

Andromeda's Daughter

Gay Guard-Chamberlin

I was angry with my mother
back when she was a woman
chained to her shopping cart
like Andromeda to her rock.

I walked behind, a sullen spy
in someone else's court,
her exhausted walk
my first close-up look at lack.

Her stingy shoes clicked in time
with the one wobbly wheel,
making a jarring tune
I wanted to never learn.

She seemed a drudge
bludgeoned into service,
a cowering dog
drifting toward traffic.

How I hated her then,
hated the endless lists
clenched in her fist,
but it was that metal cart

I loathed most of all, the way it,
after the groceries were put away,
folded in on itself with a snap,
and into the corner was hung.

Photo by Enid Fefer

The Illusion of Energy

Gay Guard-Chamberlin

I like to imagine myself
Like some ancient deity reborn,
But the more I try to multitask
The more frantic is my dance.

Still, I try to hold it all
With the decorum of the divine:
Laptop, journal, one old cat,
Cell phone, teapot, spoons,

Steering wheel, scissors, keys,
Library books, three remotes,
Laundry overflowing,
Paintbrushes, potted plants...

I do my best to juggle
But, once again, I fumble.

Gay Guard-Chamberlin is a poet-artist living in the Devon neighborhood. Marshall McLuhan, philosopher and cultural critic ("the medium is the message") once called her "Mini/Maxi." Her life has never been quite the same. Gay's work can also be found in her book, *Red Thread Through a Rusty Needle*.

Photo by Carol Beu

The Almighty Matzo Ball

Trudi Goodman

Where did all the real matzo balls go? I ask myself this question on special occasions...Jewish holidays, Friday night dinners, and times when I need comfort food. Matzo balls from restaurants never got rave reviews from me. Why? Because a matzo ball that is the shape and size of a football is obscene. Two inches in diameter and round is adequate. This dimension has been in place for centuries. Besides the particular size, it should be firm but not too chewy and not gray, but more of an off-white. I imagine the secret of the matzo ball having been carried across the desert and beyond. Wherever Jewish people made their home, the recipe moved right in.

Recently, I had Rosh Hashanah dinner at a cousin's house. In the many conversations that took place, the possibility of she and her husband selling their house and downsizing to a condo was discussed. Her nine-year-old grandson was listening in and asked, "But, Bubbe, if you move, who will make the matzo balls?"

At that moment, I realized the reason there were no more genuine matzo balls was that the maker had moved on. She left this world and took with her the instructions for making this delicacy. There is a need for the exact amounts of each ingredient and a mental image of the handling. The hands hold the key, the tender touch to forming a perfect ball. What about the soup the matzo balls live in? Who can be trusted without the original recipe the Bubbes brought with them when they came sailing over the ocean to America?

Bubbe (the Yiddish word for grandma) never left the kitchen except for on Saturday, her day to pray and rest, the Jewish Sabbath. However, by Sunday she was busy over a hot stove once again throwing herself into chopping, cutting, stirring with unbelievable energy one would not expect from a dainty petite woman of probably 100 pounds, who stood four feet eleven inches tall (maybe five feet in her black lace-up shoes).

She was forever dressed in a swirl with a long apron covering it. Her gray hair permanently pulled back in a tight round bun that sat on top of her head was shiny and perfect. Makeup was never painted on her sweet, clear complexion that surrounded her gentle green-blue eyes. She looked somewhat like the woman in the painting American Gothic by Grant Wood, except Bubbe spoke Yiddish.

"What's in a matzo ball?" I asked.

"A little schmaltz and a little gribenes. Kinder, are you paying attention?" Bubbe warned me.

This keeper of all Jewish recipes never wrote them down. "They come from my head." Bubbe would say.

My first memories of her begin when I was about five or six, and where else but at the kitchen table in her apartment she shared with a married son, a married daughter with a son, and a boarder. Her husband, my grandfather, died when I was five. Chicken soup was a daily staple, as was challah. The fragrance from her cooking that traveled from room to room throughout the apartment was like an aphrodisiac.

"We're here at Bubbe's. Can you smell it? Get a whiff," my dad would announce.

The entrance to the apartment held telltale odors of what was ahead of us. No one in the building seemed to mind; the smell confirmed the presence of life.

While I sat at the table watching her knead dough, she paid little attention to me. Her concentration and loyalty to the process took over, and she was a master cook of the Jewish persuasion. The challah was her focus. The braided dough at the top of the "staff of life" got a glistening surface with brushed-on egg white. Bubbe then covered the bread with a dish cloth and delivered the unbaked loaf to the top of a heated radiator. It had to rise because it was under the influence of yeast. By that time her soup was bubbling wildly, and the matzo balls were ready to dive right in.

When Bubbe had to leave her kitchen, she did so with grace and quiet. That was her style throughout her life. She and her recipes passed on at age 96.

My big regret is not having paid attention to what was important in life. Maybe if I had, the matzo ball would have been saved.

Photo by Robynne Wallace

Flying Up High with Some Guy in the Sky
Is My Idea of Something to Fear

Trudi Goodman

After two and a half hours in the sky, my plane arrives. This, for me, is perfection exemplified. I sigh with relief, and my white knuckles release their grip on the arm rests. I laugh, "Ha, ha, what was I worried about? Silly me."

My sense of well-being is overwhelming. Even the embarrassing moment I have when I'm the only one applauding doesn't take away the happiness enveloping me. I try to remain in control of my joy. Can't be too optimistic. Might jinx it as the plane is still taxiing in! While flying high in the sky, I looked around at the passengers. Some were sleeping, several snoring blissfully; others read, quietly turning pages as if they were in a library. Some ordered drinks. Should I have suggested, "One is enough, people. Get a grip. Stay sober to help with the evacuation."? They didn't seem to be bothered by the possibility of crashing or exploding or dropping into a lake, river, or highway.

No one really cares about my fear. They say, "Listen lady, if your time's up, it's up."

While living in Germany, my husband and I took many trips, some in a car and some in the air. On one of our plane trips, five nuns sat across from us. They spoke not a word to each other the entire time we were in the air. The ladies held beautiful rosaries, bowed their heads, and muttered prayers to themselves as they touched each precious bead. Even though I'm far from religious and Jewish, I was very thankful for this vision in black and white and felt indebted to them when we landed. There was a mystery about their intensity—as if they knew something I didn't. Perhaps their concern was imminent and their devotion was being tested. I tried to find out what order they belonged to. I needed to write a them thank you note to encourage their process for subsequent flights, but alas, I was unable to locate the miraculous ladies.

There was a time when I considered taking a seminar on "What Keeps The Plane Up" (the mechanical explanation of a plane and other sundry and popular or unpopular questions) to help conquer my fear. In the end, being more informed about the mechanics of the plane didn't appeal to me. The pressure, yes the pressure, and the responsibility put upon me would have been mind boggling. What if I'd taken the class? Then I might feel the need to peer into the plane's engine before takeoff to look for a screw or bolt or a loose whatchamacallit. And what if it had never been worked on? Skipped over like the six-foot muscle-bound passenger who, untouched by plastic glove–covered hands, passed through security while an 84-year-old, five foot one–inch, one hundred fifteen–pound woman got pulled over for inspection. Yes, that was me. Is that fair?

I handle my fear of flying by staying awake so I can inform the pilot and crew if there is smoke or the engine falls off the plane. The other passengers can sleep if they want to. Anyway, I'm better working alone.

My flying fear doesn't end with just concern for myself. I've extended it to all family members and good friends. I secretly go through a tedious investigations to secure information on their departures and arrivals.

I still have a few flights left in me, and if I were smart I'd get myself a rosary.

Photo by Enid Fefer

Packing My Suitcase

Trudi Goodman

At a very young age I decided I was adopted. I became fascinated with the story of Cinderella, and it soon became my reality. Like Cinderella, I too cleaned house, shopped for food, and wore hand-me-downs. My fairy-godmother was my grandmother who lived with us. She was always on my side but to no avail. Her residence ended when I was twelve years old. She fled to California.

One clue that I was adopted stayed with me for a long time. It came from my sad attempts at running away from home. I first tried at the age of eight or nine. I wish I could remember why I was leaving home—I'm almost positive it had something to do with my younger sister, the one born two years after me. My parents always took her side of every story, every conflict, and every fight, and I'd had enough.

That was it. "Mom I'm running away from home. I know I'm adopted and no one wants me."

"Can I help you pack?" Mom shouted from the kitchen.

I knew it, I knew it. There was the proof. I was adopted!

I put together some clothes in a child's play suitcase, took a quarter from my piggy bank, and at seven in the evening started down the stairs of my apartment to the sidewalk at 824 North Springfield and walked up to the corner of Chicago Avenue to sit. Yes, I just sat. I had nowhere to go.

Mother didn't follow me. More proof. She'd be sorry if I were kidnapped. I'd be sorry if I were kidnapped. I sat on the curb staring into the black night, focusing on the imaginary kidnapper and decided it would be better to run away in the morning. Still, I had no idea where I would run to. As luck would have it, morning came and so did school. I was literally saved by the bell.

My declaration of running away on the various occasions when I felt mistreated and totally ignored became a family ritual along with chicken every Sunday. And, that was that. The truth was, chicken dinner was more important in the scheme of things. I was second in line to a chicken.

By the time I was in high school, my thoughts of leaving home ceased to exist—well sorta. My problems with my sister ended. I just made up my mind not to talk to her. And, for ten years that worked.

Thoughts about how I became a Dinitz (my maiden name) never left and every so often nagged at me until one day after my parents died. I was talking on the phone to a cousin when my suspicions were confirmed. I wasn't destroyed by the news of my illegitimacy as much as I was struck by the fun my cousin was having telling the story. Too much fun!

"Your mother's father came to your father's house with a shotgun—and so the story goes—and you were present at the marriage. A shotgun wedding. What? You didn't know?"

That was, after all, 1934. What would you expect? It was at the end of the Depression with World War II coming; nothing was easy. Mom and Dad became my parents when they were very young, Mom 17 and Dad 19. I never had any thoughts about which came first, their marriage or my carriage. Finally, when I was about fifty, my cousin spilled the beans. I found out everyone in the family knew the story but me and my siblings. Although, I'd always had my suspicions, my thoughts had led me to believe I was adopted. Never had I suspected that I was, oh, how I hate this word, a BASTARD baby. It's hard to imagine my parents being so irresponsible.

I pictured my parents stuck in roles they played too early in their lives. My very being was an obstacle and a burden because they could hardly take care of themselves. But most importantly, all their dreams ended when I was born. I felt sad for them and I wished that they had been able to share their story and had not been so wrapped up in what was deemed a shameful situation. And who deemed this shameful anyway? There was never a time growing up that the word love was shared. I truly have no idea if they cared for me, but the secret stole their show.

However, we did behave as one would expect a loving family to act. Grandchildren were born, family dinners were served, birthdays and holidays were celebrated, special occasions recognized, and there were disagreements.

When I said goodbye to my cousin after hearing the story of my conception, I felt relieved. All the stories I'd told myself about my place in the family made sense. My child intuition was confirmed.

Photo by Donna Pecore

The Telephone—Past And Present

Trudi Goodman

The phone routine, back in the day, went like this: An operator on a switchboard responded with a high-spirited voice saying, "Number please!" A nickel or a slug was inserted into a telephone box, and magically you were connected to a friend or family member. Their words passed through wind, snow storms, thunder storms, trees, buildings, and, of course, special wiring for which we could all thank the genius of Alexander Graham Bell.

Growing up, we had a two-party line available to five family members. The circumstances limited my phone time to one call a night for 10 minutes, and not a minute more. My mother stood over me like an army sergeant to make sure I was off the phone in the exact amount of time required.

How many times during my teenage years did I hear "GET OFF THE PHONE. TIME'S UP—YOU TALKED ENOUGH." Mother's voice had a strength that could pull the phone right out of the wall. It always reminded me of Sofie Tucker or Ethel Merman. I never understood what she meant by ENOUGH. What's enough talk? Her rules about phone calls were similar to the rules for prison inmates who stand in line desperate to talk to a loved one, and if not calls were not properly timed, there would be bounteous punishments.

In the 1940s it was a privilege to have access to a telephone, but the two-party line was not too convenient, especially when the call I needed to make was urgent. Girlfriend urgent.

Throughout the years that my family and I lived on Springfield Avenue in Chicago, my mother quite often got the urge to paint the kitchen floor. She said she was having a nervous breakdown looking at the same floor day in and day out. The fact that our kitchen was not much larger than the famous kitchen on "The Honeymooners" TV show made the project not too difficult.

She was pregnant with my youngest sister when she decided to paint the floor in the artistry of Jackson Pollock. Different cans of house paint were lined up for the event. Red, blue, green, white, yellow, and purple. Each got its turn to be splashed with a big brush over the entire linoleum floor creating a marbleized effect. It took two days or more to dry, which meant no entry to the kitchen, no cooked dinners, and no phone available until we were able to walk on the floor. She went into labor soon after the do-over.

At Michael Reese hospital, Mom delivered an eleven-pound baby girl, and I was put in charge of informing Father.

"Hi Dad, it's a girl! Now you have three girls Dad! Isn't that nice Dad?"

CLICK!

"BUT DAD, don't you want to know how things are?"

My first hang-up.

After my mother came home with my baby sister, she had a nervous breakdown and landed back in the hospital. Besides having to help take care of the baby, I had complete control of the phone. I took delight in calling everyone I knew to tell them of our latest addition to the family. No one else hung up.

I can't remember my last days with a party line or using slugs and nickels to be connected to someone or when our wall phone was replaced with a dial phone and the operator became extinct. It all just seemed to happen.

And then came call waiting! I felt like a switchboard operator when that feature came along. I had children at that time, and I was what I considered to be not just a stay-at-home mom, but a shut-in. Yes, I was a shut-in. The phone became more powerful than I could ever have imagined. The 15 or so foot wire attached to the receiver came in handy. Without skipping a beat, I was able to do a little dusting, perhaps some cooking, and I definitely was able to take a walk from the kitchen to the bathroom to the living room and back to the kitchen. That curly wire was my lifeline.

Soon after I moved into my home in Morton Grove with my husband and three children, my father would just drop in on me—no warning. He and my mother lived close by in Skokie, and for some reason, his route to anywhere ended or began with my house.

I knew he was nervous about how things were working in my house, as he was with all his children. Was I paying attention to the fire regulations? For some reason he anticipated seeing my house on fire and drove by just to give his wild imagination a rest.

"I was in the neighborhood so thought I'd stop by." Luckily, the phone cord stretched to the back door where he always entered.

I figured since this was my house, my phone, my kitchen, and my phone bill I could use the phone any time I chose to. Just because my father decided to visit me any time he chose to didn't mean I had to give up my connection with the outer world. It is important to know that my father hated the telephone. His only admitted use for it was for betting on the horses. He also had a friend who he supported in hiding a phone for him in his own store—the guy was a bookie.
His own calls, whenever he made them, always had a question. "Hello, how's everything working in the house? New refrigerator running OK? Good—good." Click!

"Don't you ever get off the phone? It's like it's connected to your ear." With that he'd bang the back door so I'd know he was leaving.

The day I got a message machine was one for celebration. Call waiting, message recordings and a 15-foot curly wire. All mine!

When the kids were almost out of college, I decided to go back to work. With the job came a suggestion that I get a cell phone, the new style of communication. I wanted nothing to do with this instrument of the times. Land lines were fine with me, and I really didn't trust the cell. I knew it would take me some time to figure out how to use one, and it didn't seem worth the investment. When I finally gave in to getting one—because I was teased into it—I made a vow that I would use it only in an emergency.

I learned how to dial and get connected to another phone—I was fine with my limited knowledge. My still-in-existence land line was there leaving me feeling secure. Other possible benefits of the cell were going to remain a mystery to me. As for texting, when that came into the picture, I knew there was no way.

One night when I was entertaining some family members, one of my cousins suggested that I try to use more of the functions of my cell. He was playing around with my phone when suddenly he burst into laughter. When he finally caught his breath, he asked me in a very serious tone, "What are you planning to do with the 150 or so pictures you have taken of your ear?"

So, that was the click I heard every time I made a call.

I went along with the entire room laughing at me and remember thinking that this was great material for the storytelling at parties. I could just blurt out my ignorance and everyone would say, "Oh, that is so funny. What a funny story!" I love those words.

It all changed, when, some years later, my cousin repeated the story to my family. My daughter kept a blank look throughout the entire tale. My grandchildren laughed hysterically. After everyone else left, my daughter told me that the story was the most idiotic thing she'd ever heard, that she in no way thought it was funny, that maybe I needed to rethink my sense of humor, and so on.

There are narratives still waiting to be told in the crossroads of a million private lives. Funny, sad, and romantic tales will float freely across wires or wirelessly through the air.

Should Parents Be Allowed to Name Their Babies?

Trudi Goodman

When I was born, my mother named me Toba Eve, a request from my great aunt. After two weeks, she got into an argument with the aunt, and he next day, my name was changed. From that day forward, I have been known as Trudith Joyce Toba Eve Dinitz. Nickname, Trudi. And, with my names came this convoluted story.

Mom and I had to walk a mile from our apartment on Springfield Avenue in Chicago to a large red brick building, Ryerson Elementary school, on Lawndale Avenue, to register me for first grade. At the very start of the process there was already a problem. Mom told the registrar why I have four names, the reason just two appear on my birth certificate, that I'm to be called Trudy, short for Trudith, and to ignore the birth certificate name Toba. Confused? Me too! I can imagine the registrar's head spinning! Why couldn't my parents just have gone to court for a name change like normal people do? My mother came up with this ruse so she could get by with all the names that were bestowed upon me. She figured no one at that time, 1940, knew much about Judaism, and a little white lie wouldn't hurt. So, she told the registrar that the name on my birth certificate was my Hebrew name and that's what Jewish people did—they put their Hebrew names on their birth certificates. But she said she preferred an American name for her daughter. The woman in charge showed definite signs of confusion, holding her head and blinking rapidly. I was finally signed in. Trudy was the name I was called. Later, in high school, just to complicate matters, I dropped the y and changed it to an i...Trudi.

Because my parents never went to court to change my birth certificate, I carry the tremendous burden of five surnames. American names: Trudith Joyce. Hebrew names: Toba Eve. Nickname: Trudi. All five names followed me through school. The paperwork that went into just recording my names probably used up half a tree and hours of manpower, all because my parents avoided the legal process.

My last name came with its own set of problems. Dinitz is my maiden name. The name prompted many jokes that followed me throughout school.

"So, your name is Trudi Donuts."

"Did you say Trudi Dimwitz?"

Lovely huh? I well deserved my married name—Goodman. Simple. A combo of two highly respected words in the English language. Maybe I would have changed the man part to woman.
Goodwoman, YES. Goodwoman—that's even better, isn't it?

Trudi Goodman is a former interior designer and a grandmother to four girls and one boy. She resides in the suburbs and has enjoyed being a member of the Budlong

Woods writers' group more than she can say. Her creative self is much more confident when painting since she's been in the visual arts for most of her life. Writing has shown Trudi another way to create but still remains a mighty challenge.

Photo by Carol Beu

Lola's Jar

Ofelia C. Hamper

Lola's or grandma's jar
part of kitchen counter
I've seen like no other
as a child until today.

Palest beige
sandy shade
smooth surface
polished porcelain.

A foot standing
eight-inch diameter
so simple and plain
unassuming luster.

Just a white-rock-salt jug
unlike child's clear cookie jar
then for ocean's rich harvest
now, fish with sodium in supermarket.

Today, Lola's jar is empty
while it sits content
on sis's art shelf, pretty
 piece of history.

Photo by Daelyn Frasier

Loose Pendant

Ofelia C. Hamper

My loose pendant
inverted heart–shaped
blue faux aquamarine
crystal, clear, translucent.

A flare for some time
reminds me of Titanic
Rose's Heart of the Ocean
mine misses a chain to slide in.

Have always wanted to wear
but couldn't find a necklace
need not be platinum or silver
perhaps rope, yarn or fiber

Finally, I found a bargain:
a plain stainless chain.

Photo by Carol Beu

Wedding Watch

Ofelia C. Hamper

Bride: Why do you need
         a new wristwatch
         for our wedding?

Groom: Though I haven't seen it yet,
         you got a gorgeous flowing gown.

Bride: Can't wait to wear it!

Groom: My white shirt and bowtie
         midnight blue pants and tuxedo
         rented from men's store.

         At least, I'd own this wristwatch
         to remember our event by
         for the rest of our lives.

Bride: Fair enough, ring and watch
         makes sense maybe
         don't know, silly you,
         why I love you.

Ofelia C. Hamper began to discover the joy of writing in grade school. For her, nothing is more delightful than turning the pages as she reads through fiction and non-fiction. The best treasures are bible stories, historical manga or graphic novels, movies on rhapsody, comedy, and drama with stylish lines of epic poetry.

Photo by Liz Barton

His Lips

Susan Hernandez

His lips
Oh, his lips
So soft, full, sweet
Luscious-looking lips
When he speaks
I watch his lips in motion
And my body tingles
My mouth waters
And I am filled with emotions
Those lips, his
Do not belong to me
But to her
As
I have a pair of my own
Oh but
Wouldn't it be so nice
If his lips could be on loan
For just one starlit
Moonlit night
But, it just isn't right
To cross the married zone
And to venture into
Lips unknown
His lips are full of
Heaven and hell
I just want to place
My lips on his
Spreading them apart with my own
So I could feel his
Wet mouth on mine
Kissing them
Sucking them
Devouring them
Until his body longs for more
Isn't that what a fantasy is for?

Evolution

Susan Hernandez

From a voluptuous woman
she grew big and fat
but was not quite
used to that
but was secure in its armor
Few
now challenged to have their
way with her
and the ones that did
she was confident
to handle
She was no longer
a peanut in a shell
but the
Nutcracker

Photo by Enid Fefer

Who Is She

Susan Hernandez

Who is she
or
Who is she meant to be
This woman with no bravery
Down on her knees
She begs and she pleads
But, they do not understand
her family, nor man
Trapped in a role she has long outgrown
Her mind is filled with misery
as is her body, cramped in agony
Yet her heart still pumps the blood
of family and love
Blue before the air, it circulates her veins
Blue is the color of her love
feeling so unworthy of red hot passion
wanting so much more but
not knowing how to open the door
to stand on her own
She remains
paralyzed
 in a role
she has long outgrown

Original Artwork by Tony Pigott

Breathe

Susan Hernandez

Today I almost let you infuriate me
You moved my things around
like you always do
a game you love to play
But today
I took a breath and gave it thought
I don't want to play these games with you
I finally realized
I don't have to
Now a smile on my face
and some peace in my mind
now knowing
I never have to work overtime
I feel rested and the best is
this is the way it can always be for me
Breathe

Susan Hernandez, Chicago-born poet and artist, writes what her soul feels. The way that words can make her cry or laugh amazes her. She loves that she can write a poem, read it on stage and know that the audience feels it. Susan was once honored by David Hernandez when he asked her to share the Chicago Cultural Center's stage with him. Words have so much power, and every letter from A to Z is her best friend. The only thing more important than poetry and art to Susan is family.

Photo by Carol Beu

What I Saw Today at Starbucks

Betty Jacobsen

what I saw today at Starbucks was this
a long red scarf in the parking lot
blown by a bitter wind then
trapped beneath my tires
a copper penny as I entered
gleaming brightly on the floor
and through the window
snowflakes falling against a smeary sky
bare tree branches wildly trembling

two slim young men in biking gear
all black and sleek like sea creatures
stride through the entrance
in full command of their shiny bodies
they order eat and promptly depart
leaving behind an unpleasant blast
of icy air from the opened door

beside me a woman young or youngish
slumps seeming senseless in her chair
then stands then stumbles then falls to the floor
from drink perhaps or drugs or a life too hard
I leave my chair to help her rise
she slurring thanks me for my hand
and tells me she'd just been dreaming
of God's son reaching out to her

the penny shines now in my pocket
tonight I'll wash the long red scarf
tomorrow it will warm me
as the coffee did today
I worry though about the falling woman
who reeled out the door alone
into the dimming light
of the winter afternoon

Unzip That Bag

Betty Jacobsen

unzip that bag of words
with meanings taut
and untaught
spill them onto the page
like ripe fruit or seed searching
for a fertile rooting place where
words will grow under the bluing sky
blow on the winding wind whirling
up the crazy crags of mountain heights
heigh ho hi ho
hi who do you think you are
no why do you think
you are

digging there through the mound
of unsorted words illusory locutions
rooting rummaging snuffing about
in the mean meanings of your average day
fraught with the frightening sense
of where or where
is the end of time
the beginning of thyme
the rose of mary the lavender scent
to clear the head of nonsleep
and coax dreams
from the fog of day
into the clarity of night
where words released from the unzipped bag
spin and skip and weave themselves
into shimmering kaleidoscope visions

I Thought I Would Write About

Betty Jacobsen

I thought I would write about
a saxophone in the night
dandelions in a spring lawn
the squirrel that runs past my window
each morning on his telephone wire highway

or about a walk by the lake
on a sunny May afternoon and
the young couple launching a kite
a sudden wind takes from them
or the handsome men intimately lolling
at the end of the beach
they call their own
the empty water bottle along the shore
waiting the next wave
or maybe about the marble eyed
stare of a gull as I passed

then I thought perhaps I would write about
the incomprehensible words you murmured
through barely moving lips as you
turned and closed the door behind you
but in the end I wrote about
nothing at all

Photo by Robynne Wallace

List of First Loves

Betty Jacobsen

My first love was Tarzan. He lived in a tree house with Jane and Boy and Cheetah, the chimp. He could talk with the apes and ride elephants and swing through the trees on jungle vines. I wanted to go to Africa and live with him in the trees. I was so in love with Tarzan. I wanted to BE Tarzan. I would strip and look at myself in my bedroom mirror and hope I would never never ever ever grow breasts.

My first love was Rex. He was a twin. His brother's name was Max. We were in first grade. We learned a dance for a school performance. I so wanted to impress him. But during the performance I fell and skinned my knees and bled on the floor. I jumped right back up but was obliterated by embarrassment. Rex moved back to Kentucky soon after that. Max too.

My first love was a German boy. A young man really. Maybe his name was Kurt. He lived for some months on the farm behind ours. Many nights the winter he lived there, I would kneel at my window, nearly opaque with frost lace and raise the small louver in the frame below the glass to let in the cold night air. I would put my mouth to the opening, breathe out my prayers in the direction of his farm and watch them turn white in the icy air. I would breathe out my prayers so intensely I was sure they would reach him and he would soon come to carry me away into forever.

My first love was Hamlet. Well, Sir Lawrence Olivier as Hamlet. I saw the movie at the theater in the town seven miles down the road. I adored him. I wanted to learn ballet so I could impress him. I wanted to dance like the ballerina in The Red Shoes, which I saw in the same theater the same year. I knew I'd never meet him. All the same. I would imagine he was impressed by my beauty and grace, and I would dance myself to death for him like the Red Shoes ballerina.

My first love was a cousin who came from Denmark to live with us for a while. I was 13 maybe. He was about 12 years older and spoke English with a Danish accent. So cute. He had a wonderful sense of humor and was always playing practical jokes. Once, two young women were trying very hard to get a date with him. He finally invited each of them out for a date. The same date. He picked one up. Then the other. He took them both to a movie and afterward for ice cream. I don't think either ever again spoke to him. He eventually married a Southern belle. They moved to Tennessee where, in fairly short order, she found horses and other men more interesting and he became a bigot.

My first love was Janie. But only after we moved to the farm. She had been my best friend in elementary school before the farm. Janie and her family came to the country one time to visit us. I remember having odd, uneasy feelings I didn't understand. Like maybe I was in love with her. Or something like that. Maybe. We were in the barn and had climbed the ladder to the hay mow. We sat on the high mow floor leaning against prickly bales of freshly cut hay. Our legs dangled over the edge.

We looked down at the green and yellow John Deere below our feet. We didn't talk much. The smell of hay and mouse was in the air. I felt an intense desire to kiss her. It was powerful. Almost uncontrollable. It filled my entire mind. It almost blinded me. But I knew it would be the end of our friendship if I did and that it would be a line I couldn't uncross. I don't recall ever wanting to kiss another girl. Go figure.

My first love was a boy in high school whose name I don't remember. He sat a few rows in front of me. I don't recall which class. I looked at the back of his head for months. And loved him. And loved him. And longed for him to love me. I don't remember his face. Just the back of his head. His hair was reddish blond. I have no idea why I was attracted to him. I never spoke to him. He never looked at me.

My first love was Robert Hoffman. Well, he wasn't a first love at all. In fact I hardly noticed him. But maybe I was one of his. I believe he had a crush on me. He was in my high school home room. We sat near each other because of the alphabet. Some time near the end of our senior year or very shortly thereafter I received a letter from him. He was in prison. I don't know for what and I don't remember what he wrote except that he asked me to write to him. I didn't. I don't know why I didn't. Maybe I was a little scared. I wish now I had. He must have felt lonely and afraid. He was just a kid. Quiet and not bad looking. I don't know what became of him but somehow I do think of him more often than one might expect. And always with regret for the unanswered letter.

My first love was a teenage boy. Thirteen or 14 maybe. But I was more like 30. I was taking a two-week Spanish course in Mexico and was a bit lonely and disoriented. He was the son of my host family and had time each day to help me learn the language. We lay on the rooftop one evening looking at the stars. Something began to stir between us. But I was the adult, right? I gently excused myself and went back to my room. Before I returned to the US, he gave me a small silver coin as a memento of our friendship. Sweet.

There were later loves too. Fine loves all. Though not memorable in the same light delicate way of these early ones..

But my first real love, my real first love, memorable in every detail, my only first love, my true and forever first love is John whom I met as he stood against a dark window in a tall building on a cold winter night almost 40 years ago. And that was that.

Bunny Redux

Betty Jacobsen

A juvenile rabbit, just recently out on his own
visits my garden each afternoon around three.
He snacks while I have tea.
He and his rabbity ilk live 'neath my next neighbor's porch.
I'm guessing so anyway
'cause he always appears from that general direction
emerging ever so promptly each day
from betwixt purple phlox and blue balloon flowers.
I sit in my green Adirondack and glower.

Oh, he's cute, alright. No doubts about it.
Damned cute. An adorable toy.
With his petite translucent pink pointy ears
his spotlessly white little powder puff tail.
And that singularly mobile tiny brown nose.
Also, his whiskers are quite truly charming.
But I am finding his habits increasingly alarming.
I certainly am. Yes. I am. Yes I am.

Do I mind that he nibbles the clover and grass?
No, not a bit. There's plenty of each in the yard.
Do I care that he munches a few strawberry leaves?
No, not at all. I'm willing to share.
Even a mouthful of pert portulaca? No prob.
It grows like a weed and bounces right back.
But when he fells all nine stalks of my deep azure aster
in my small city garden now that's a disaster?
Come on now, Bunny. Gimme a break.

I won't stand for it. Or sit for it, either.
Even in my comfy green chair out here on the lawn.
So. What should I do? Should I shoot 'im or poison 'im?
What do you think? Shall I borrow a rifle and off 'im at dawn?
No. Better not. Probably bring the police.
And poison I'm afraid would do in the cats.
A trap might handle it. Yeah, have a heart, maybe.
Naw, traps are too iffy. And might snare a possum
a creature that's ugly and fearsome and awesome.
And I'd have to tote the dang hissy creature
out to some far forest preserve to release 'im.

No, really. I need some assistance. I can't do it alone.
I need resolution. Do you have a solution?

I long for some peace, for the presence of calm
for a state of tranquility out on my lawn
specifically I crave, most entirely and completely
for an absolutely, total, incontrovertible
positively definite absence of Bunny.

Original Art by Dan Cleary

What Is the Answer

Betty Jacobsen

what is the answer
to the question we all ask
even if unconsciously
when the first hot day
of summer steams mushrooms
out of the damp earth and
the pale blossoms of a cool spring have
all been blown away
by last night's storm

when the vivid sturdy flowers
of summer have not yet
come forth and the lake shore
is still strewn with winter's flotsam
when only the occasional
bottle cap or cigarette end speaks of
sunbathers yet to come and this year's
serious sand castles' architects
are still making plans

perhaps the question is more
interesting than the answer
what question comes to your
mind then regarding that interim
that betweeness when spring
has not quite finished and
summer hardly begun

Photo by Carol Beu

How Long Is Forever

Betty Jacobsen

the forever of a volcano
active or not active
or of a rock or a continent
is not the same forever
as your forever or mine
though in a way of course
they are certainly related
sharing as they do
a kind of foreverishness
bounded as they are
by existence and non-existence
by here and not here
and that by the way
implies something about space
which also may or may not
have a beginning or an end

science we hope will tell us one day
what space is and what forever means
and if there is more than one of either
in the meanwhile the vow
I will remember you forever
is not much of a promise
and in any case
even if forever extends
from today until neither I
nor anyone else
knows what today is
forever is not really all that long
and the time between now
and the end of forever
is presumably
becoming shorter
by the minute

Betty Jacobsen writes to stay in contact with whatever sanity remains within herself and in this world. Betty enjoys the sense of losing herself while doing so. She also enjoys finding herself in the company of other writers as they explore together various ways to hang on.

Life of the Potato

Philomena Kilcourse

Farmer Ted Smith grows his own potatoes every year.

When he grows his potatoes, he cuts one potato into two halves. They are called slits.

He sets the slits 10 inches apart in the soil in early spring.

Three months later he digs up the potatoes.

"I'm Spud. What's your name?"

"I'm Kerr Pink."

"I feel, because we left our friends, like the worms in the soil," lamented Spud.

"Yes, but now we've to deal with these humans. They're in charge, and we're at their mercy," groaned Kerr Pink anxiously. "Will they dress us up like Cabbage Patch Dolls?"

"No, but we have to feed the world, and people need our type of food to stay alive," declared Spud.

"Are people going to cook us as fries or hash browns, microwave us in our jackets, or peel off our skin?" said the worried Kerr Pink.

"Yes, but we won't feel any pain. We don't have heartbeats, organs, nerves, muscles, or blood running through our veins because we have none," assured Spud.

"We have no bones or back bone, so we can't speak up for ourselves with the humans. What will we do?" snapped Kerr Pink.

"We can become chopped liver," chuckled Spud.

"If people peel away my pink jacket, I won't be able to wear pink and pink is my favorite color. I feel so sad," wailed Kerr Pink.

"Don't worry. You're a Kerr Pink potato. If you flip a pancake, it's still a pancake. Ha! Ha! Ha!" laughed Spud.

"Oh, Spud, you make me feel so happy. Hungry people can butter us up. We would be very tasty indeed," laughed Kerr Pink in a relaxed mood.

"If people were very hungry for our type of food, they would gain weight. Ha! Ha! Ha!" laughed Spud.

"Some people never cook right," sighed Kerr Pink.

"Right," said Spud.

"We're going to Grandma's for the holidays, and she makes real good potato salad. It's awesome," babbled Kerr Pink.

"Yes, we get to meet our cousins, sweet potatoes, and they're as sweet as pie," gushed Spud.

"People love to party, especially round the holidays. If people spilled wine on us, we would shrivel up like our friends the worms. Oh dear, what would we do if that happened?" cried Kerr Pink.

"Join the party and get drunk like people do! Ha! Ha! Ha!" giggled Spud.

"That's not funny!" yelled Kerr Pink. "Oh I'm so confused." She paused. "We don't know whose home we'll end up in."

"No, we don't. Humans growl at us when they're hungry. They don't care if we wear a jacket or not," Spud said with a smile. "Farmers grow new potatoes every year."

Photo by Donna Pecore

Obscurity After Life

Philomena Kilcourse

Numb are the mummies
Silent is their kind
Wrapped up in bandages
That's what you will find

They wear the clothes of culture
To the end of time
No need for modern fashion
No clothes to spend a dime

No movement where they lay
No wave of a hand
No glance at each other
No name can they brand

No ringing bells they hear
No footsteps, no sound
Never a movement
Even when people are around

Original Artwork by Daniel Cleary

The Mysteries of God's Love

Philomena Kilcourse

Although You are a mystery
And You have all the fame
As we turn away from You
Our eyes we need to train

For You have many names
Father, Son, and Holy Spirit
We give You thanks
For You have all the merit

For You are majestic
Singing praises up above
You died upon the cross
While sharing us Your love

As we go to Mass each day
For You are present there
We can only find love in You
Because in You we share

We can only love You
As there is no other
You give Yourself to us
As a sister and a brother

As we shed a tear each day
This is a gift from You
Suffering draws us closer
The crosses we bear too

You are present in the Host
We celebrate together
Knowing that it comes from You
Our burdens are a feather

You suffered for the world
Bravely You have won
For those who share eternity
Others from You did run

Although You are majestic
While there is no other
You want to share Your blessings

You want to share Your mother

When our tongues are full of praises
The blessings You prepared
To share with all of us
Your body was not spared

For we can only love You
When we are close to You
We can know Your present
The joy that we have too

We can thank You every day
The journey that we travel
The ups and downs are many
The joy You give, we marvel

While You hung upon the cross
Your bones they did not break
Your side was pierced that day
Blood and water were not fake

You send blessings from above
With many different gifts
For we are all connected
Within our heart, it lifts

Mercy Sunday is for all
Your mercy is divine
my greatest wish for everyone
throughout the world You shine

I long to share You every day
With many empty hearts
Because Your mercy is so great
we want to be a part

Your heart is ready to forgive
Your heart gives us joy
So we can have peace on earth
For each girl and boy

No matter when You touch our hearts
Whatever time it be
We receive You in our lives
To join You eternally

Philomena Kilcourse loves to listen to *Owen Mac*, a young singer from Ireland. He inspires her to further her artistic and literary pursuits. Writing helps her express her feelings. Philomena smiles when she hears *Owen Mac's* extraordinary voice, which has her reminiscing of Ireland.

Photo by Enid Fefer

Finding Seasonal Help

Richard Kimball

"How many more do we have?" he asked as he pulled another application from the pile.

April munched on a carrot before she replied, "Only three more today, sir."

"Sheesh! I hate this time of year," he muttered. "Why are there so many openings this year?"

"Big bad wolves took a big bite out this time."

"How many openings do we have left?"

"Just two more. You need one for the Orthodox, but we have to fill the other one first. The hors d'oeuvres are really exemplary, don't you think?" April replied, hopping from one thought to another. She picked up a radish and started to nibble.

"Yes. The lettuce was tasty," he allowed as he skimmed the next resume. "Speaks to climate change that it is available this early in the season. Why do we need to fill the other position first?"

April sighed inwardly. He was so easily confused these days. "You are responsible for two Easters each year. The Orthodox one comes later, so you have a little more time to fill that opening," she gently reminded him.

He cocked one big white ear while he peered at her intently over his reading glasses. She had the distinct impression that he was receiving this news as if for the first time. She eyed the buffet laid out under the window and briefly debated the merits of lettuce instead of kale.

She'd served as an assistant for the Great Rabbit—or G.R. as she now affectionately called him—since before genetically modified carrots. It was hard to watch him become more hare-brained every day. While age and predators had eliminated those who were the Great Rabbit before him, her job now was to make sure that his career on the bunny trail was limited to appearances at malls and farmer's markets. As the Great Rabbit, he had the responsibility of choosing suitable assistant Easter rabbit and bunny replacements system wide—the CEO protecting the brand, as it were. She wondered how much longer he could carry on.

"Let's see the next candidate then," he sighed.

April opened the door and called out, "Mr. Tail? Peter? Next!"

Peter could best be described as a millennial rabbit. He had none of the traditional traits; his nose barely twitched, and he moved with a smooth, ballroom-inspired glide. His pink and purple plaid pants clashed with his red vest. One ear flopped over at a rakish angle, and the tip of the other just bent, barely concealing a small egg-shaped tattoo.

April glanced at the photo of G.R. and his sister Flopsy on the desk corner. G.R. used to reminisce that Flopsy could never get her ears to stand up straight either. Flopsy had not been the best judge of spousal material; she was always popping up with a new beau and brood to match.

G.R. reached for his glass of carrot juice as Peter blurted out, "You probably don't remember me sir, but my great-grandmother was Flopsy."

Shocked, G.R. spewed a mouthful of juice back into the glass. He seemed disoriented, so April gently took over. "Why do you want to be an Easter bunny?" she asked while G.R. dabbed at stray juice splatters.

"I'm good with kids and I want to carry on the family tradition," Peter said with a wink and a big smile that revealed a diamond-embedded incisor.

April eyed the dwindling pile of applications, then glanced over in time to see G.R. shudder. When he glanced at her, she gave an almost imperceptible shake of her head. G.R. responded with a slight nod of his own.

She put a paw around the stunned Peter's shoulder and lifted him from his seat. "Well, it was very nice of you to apply. Thank you so much for stopping by," she said as she marched him to the door and closed it firmly behind him. With a sigh, she turned to face G.R.

He shook his head wearily as he examined the resume again. "Peter C. Tail. Really? I suppose the C stands for Cotton!" April just shrugged. He slapped the paper face down onto the growing pile of rejects then picked up his now half-empty glass of carrot juice. April detoured by way of the buffet. He was deep in thought when she returned, a spinach stem just disappearing between her front teeth.

"How many more openings?" he asked absentmindedly.

"Two."

"And how much time do we have before Easter?"

April replied softly, "Not much longer now, sir. Not much longer now."

Richard Kimball is a retired flamingophile (the dregs of his collection are in a closet somewhere) and is in the throes of Lalique withdrawal. (While he still has some, he has avoided getting more since the Lalique family sold the business.) He has been adopted by a feral cat colony and makes sure they have food, water, and a referee at breeding time. Retired from a business career in confectionary, Richard now works part-time for the Songs By Heart Foundation, providing music for memory care units in nursing homes.

Washing Dishes

John Kirby

I suppose just about everyone has some task that they view with relish. Not that they want to do the task, but they enjoy getting it done. I have two of these tasks: washing dishes and making my bed.

I know that I am not alone in delighting in completing seemingly mundane tasks. Gregory Hines, the late dancer/actor was interviewed on the TV show 60 Minutes. Part of the interview was conducted in Mr. Hines' laundry room, where he revealed that he enjoyed folding laundry. He explained that he enjoyed the view and feeling of seeing the fruits of his efforts. I now realize that my two delights stem from the enjoyment of completing a necessary task in a particular way.

Relishing the making of my bed grew out of my consciously trying to create a habit. I had read that if you do something for three weeks, it will become a habit. I decided to give it a try. I wanted to get into the habit of making my bed as I did not enjoy the sight of a messy one. Sure enough, after three weeks I had a mild habit. In the years since, the habit has become an addiction. The last time I did not make my bed upon awakening was when I knew that I was going to wash my sheets. Why make the bed if you were only going to tear it apart in a little while?

I visited my old fraternity last year and was invited to see the new rooms, which were decided improvements over what I had to endure. But, my memory was tarnished by the universally unmade bed. The unmade bed is the image I have taken away from the visit.

At a commencement address to navy cadets, a Lieutenant Commander admonished the graduates, "First, make your bed! You will have completed one necessary task successfully and no matter how bad your day goes, you can look back at this accomplishment."

The story of washing dishes is a bit different. I believe my appreciation of it grew out of my job as a dish washer in the fraternity houses at the University of Illinois. I had received a scholarship that paid tuition and room but not board. The scholarship recipients were expected to work meal jobs. The best job was dish washer, in our view, because a good dish washer could arrive a bit late, eat a good meal, and, if he was good enough, finish the job before the waiters had left. Waiters, on the other hand, had to arrive early, wear white coats, set up, serve the main meal, clear the main dishes, serve dessert, and clear. At one frat, we dishwashers were so efficient that we would help the waiters clear the dessert dishes. We finished washing the main course dishes while the fraternity members were eating dessert.

Years later a good friend showed me the enjoyment in hosting dinner parties. I had a distinct advantage in that I had an apartment with a spectacular ocean view. I enjoyed inviting people down for dinner. I made simple meals, but always with a good salad. The best groups were those with people from different professions. Inviting all engineers was an invitation to boredom for me and most of the guests. After everyone left, I had to wash the dishes. I had to do it by hand, as the apartment was too small to be able to accommodate a dishwasher. My skills, learned in college, made the dish washing short work. And, the apartment was neat, too.

I don't mind washing dishes now. In fact, even though I now own a dish washing machine, I never use it. I've become used to washing dishes by hand, even when I have guests over. I suppose the satisfaction comes from all of the memories I have: college and the dinner parties with friends.

I know that this little essay has engendered the desire in friends and acquaintances to have me do their dishes. I will volunteer to wash dishes at someone else's party if there is a need. Of course, I'll "help" with the dishes afterwards if invited to dinner with a new and interesting group. But, I will not do all the dishes. And, no pots and pans!

Photo by Enid Fefer

A Happy Life

John Kirby

*A Happy Life: 1) Interesting Work; 2) Nice Place to Live; 3) Someone to Love
— Philosophy of Elvis Presley written on a note given to his Los Angeles hair
dresser.*

It's a simple philosophy. It took me a while after hearing it to realize how true it is.
If you had these three things, would you be happy? I came to realize that this philosophy is the foundation of having a happy, or at least satisfying, life.

Interesting Work: I had an interesting job and enjoyed it because I was learning
something new all of the time. I had progressed to the point of being considered
an expert in my field, and the job paid well. But, I never really realized the validity
of this statement until I shared it with high school students. My fellow presenter
chimed in, "I never realized it, but that is so true. I used to have a job that I hated
but paid so much that I figured I couldn't leave it. Finally, I gave up the job, and
now consider the four years I spent at that job as wasted."

We all know someone who has a job that does not pay well but loves it anyway.
When I do my presentation at high schools, I always point to the classroom teacher
and ask if they would consider another job. With two exceptions the teachers reply
that they can't think of doing something else.

Nice Place to Live: I had a head start in this category. At the time I first heard of
Elvis' philosophy, I was living in an apartment in Laguna Beach, right on the ocean.
In addition, my rent was $600 per month, including all utilities. Southern Califor-
nia is a nice place to live, but I have since realized that just about anywhere can be
a nice place to live if one is able to adapt. In Chicago, the museums, theaters, and
picturesque countryside more than make up for the weather. And, living near family
and friends is important, too. I can't remember ever living in a place that I didn't
consider nice.

Someone to Love: Can you imagine coming home knowing that the people you love
are awaiting your return? At every phase of life we seek the company of people that
we admire, respect, or just like to be around. The coffee klatch in the morning or the
group we join to learn a new skill puts us in touch with those we like, even though
we may not "love" them. Coming back from a business trip to be greeted by those I
love is one of the greatest rewards I have ever been given.

Money! It's apparent that one thing most people consider essential for a happy life
is not included in Elvis' philosophy. Since Elvis essentially had all of the money in
the world, he probably never considered it. When you think of the people you know
and their happiness, you realize that having a lot of money is not essential to happiness. But, unless you have "enough" money, the deficiency becomes an overriding
concern.

So, a corollary to Elvis' philosophy is having enough money, defined as having sufficient funds to pay next month's rent and buy food for your family, and having a reliable source of income. I should also add that enough includes putting money away for retirement. And realize that, with the stock market, just about anyone can increase their wealth substantially.

Photo by Enid Fefer

Lisa

John Kirby

Lisa Giorgi changed my life.

I first met Lisa shortly after starting work at McDonnell Douglas, an aerospace firm located in Huntington Beach, California. I rated an office all to myself, but there were no spare offices, so I was put in an area in between two offices. This was where Lisa sat. It was one of the most fortunate seating arrangements, both for me and the company.

Lisa was born on the East Coast well before World War II or "W W Roman numeral two," as Lisa used to call it. She received her PhD in English from an Eastern school just as the war ended, but I never heard her referred to as doctor by others or herself. She was a most unassuming woman.

After graduation Lisa got a job working as a clerk in the army headquarters in Paris. She married a French man. To get married in France at the time meant that she had to be tested for tuberculosis. When she reported for the test, the doctor took one look at her and ushered her out of the office with the statement, "Americans never get tuberculosis!"

She and her new husband decided to move into her larger apartment. Her rent came down immediately. When asked why, the concierge just said, "But, you are French now!"

Lisa had two children, a daughter and then a son, Charlie. Charlie was born with Down's syndrome. The delivering doctor recommended that Charlie be placed in an institution. Lisa refused and saw Charlie through eight operations to correct heart defects and other problems often associated with Down's syndrome. The doctor's prediction that Charlie would never be able to live a successful life was proven wrong when he, as a 22 year-old, labeled a picture he had drawn "C-A-T." Lisa was thrilled. There was no more talk of putting Charlie into an institution.

Lisa made it clear that if you wanted to be her friend, you would also have to be Charlie's friend. I fit into this category and found it a delight. Charlie had two passions: The Beatles and Hulk Hogan. I would occasionally meet him, and we'd have long conversations about his life and living with his mother.

***

One day, Lisa began to chuckle as she was editing a report. "Listen to this!' she exclaimed. "This is so funny." She then began to read a section of a final report. It was obvious that the author had decided to save space by using comma splices, jamming two perfectly good sentences together to shorten the report. In the process, a lot of the meaning was lost, and it was funny. But then, I sensed that the report seemed familiar. "That sounds like a report that I wrote."

Lisa sputtered, "Well, it's not really that bad."

Fortunately, I had the original hand-written copy of my input to the report. I pulled it out. Sure enough, the awkward section was mine, but the engineer to whom I had given my input had created the comma splices.

Lisa and I laughed. That, I now realize, was the true beginning of our friendship.

Under Lisa's tutelage, I became more and more interested in writing. I became a real oddity, an engineer who enjoyed writing reports.

***

Professionally, Lisa and I put out quite a few reports, I writing them and Lisa correcting them.

Then one day it happened. We got two requests for proposal (RFPs) at the same time. One was for a large contract in a new technology that our company wanted to get into. My bosses insisted that I head the proposal. The second RFP was from an East Coast government laboratory for a very small contract. I had chummed for this small contract, but because of the larger RFP, I was told I couldn't work on it. The laboratory proposal was due three days after the larger proposal. Although the laboratory contract would be small, it could lead to much bigger efforts. It was our chance to get in on the ground floor, so I wanted to pursue it.

I asked for Lisa. She had edited all of my final reports, so she knew the technology just about as well as I did. We spent half an hour going over the laboratory proposal. Then I left to work on the big proposal. When the big proposal was submitted, I went down to see Lisa.

I read her proposal. I deleted one word from Lisa's write up. We submitted the proposal and were awarded both contracts.

Lisa had another great ability. She loved to cook, a skill she learned in France. I was first introduced to her gastronomical skills at dinner party in Three Arch Bay, a small enclave right on the ocean, just south of where I lived. The meal was marvelous, as was the conversation. I began to host similar dinners. I provided steaks or spaghetti while Lisa provided the vegetable portion of the meal. We invited random guests so we would have more interesting conversation. In addition to the dinners, Lisa would occasionally host Sunday breakfasts for members of her church. I was not a member but would, on occasion, be in Huntington Beach, where Lisa lived, (25 miles from where I lived in Laguna Beach) at just the right time to partake.

Lisa told me that it was her ambition to write novels. She told me about several plots she had concocted, all of which included a disabled person like her son Charlie. He was a great guy. He used to love coming to my apartment with Lisa for our communal dinners. As I mentioned before, Charlie loved the Beatles, and I had made a two-hour long reel tape filled with Beatles songs. He would sit for hours with headphones on, bouncing to the Beatles' music.

Sadly (for me), Lisa retired and moved to St. Croix in the Virgin Islands, but even this move was not far enough to keep me away. I visited her one Thanksgiving, and dinner was incredible.

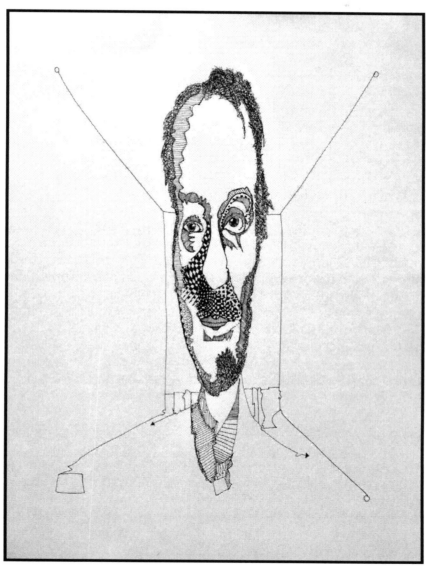

Original Artwork by Tony Pigott

George

John Kirby

The following is a true story.

I met George at the Anaheim, California Youth and Family Resource Center (YFRC), which is run by the Orange County Probation Department (OCPD). I had been a volunteer with probation, working half-days at both the YFRC and the Los Pinos Camp low-security incarceration camp for juveniles.

The purpose of the YFRC is to rehabilitate juveniles who fall into the 8% category—those at high risk for becoming career criminals. When a juvenile is picked up for a felony, they and their family members are called in for an interview. Juveniles who are judged to be at high risk for becoming career criminals are referred to the YFRC program. The county spends an estimated $1,500,000 for every juvenile who becomes a career criminal. For this reason, considerable funds are allocated for facilities to achieve rehabilitation. YFRC was run by the probation department but also had education, drug treatment, and family counseling staff.

The probation staff called the juvenile offenders clients, both because the YFRC was a shorter term and because the juveniles were indeed clients since a major goal was rehabilitation. The clients changed a lot over time as people entered and left the system or were assigned to detention facilities. So, it was not a surprise when I entered the classroom and found George. The first thing I noticed was his hair, piled three inches on top of his head like a crown. George's hair became his signature feature. He dyed it (green once), had a crew cut for a time, and, in general, seemed to experiment with his hair in a variety of ways.

It was our first meeting. I sensed his interest in me,. but I decided to ignore it for reasons I can't explain.

I never asked the juveniles why they had been incarcerated. They didn't want you to know, although they'd be more than willing to tell you why Johnny over there had been arrested. I tried to treat them with respect. Even though the POs, i.e., the probation officers, were positive role models, the clients didn't respect them because they knew POs were the enforcers. Enforcement was not in my job description.

I kept track of George, as I sensed he was different. Although we chatted only infrequently, he was always friendly, and I grew to like him.

There were blackboards in the common room, where the boys congregated for lunch, snacks and breaks. One blackboard had the names of some of the clients, each with a number after it—the number of days of detention the client had accumulated. Getting a detention was serious and the next-to-last step in the discipline chain. The number after George's name increased every time I came to the facility, which meant he was getting more than five detentions per week since he could work off one detention a day. I asked him if he could set a goal to lower the number by the next time I came in, but. he made no comment. The next week, the number was higher.

One day George was no longer at the YFRC. I found out that he'd been assigned to Los Pinos, and we saw each other the next time I went there. We proceeded to go over mathematics, the only time I ever tutored George.

Several weeks later, I saw George at the Los Pinos Administration Building, where I had to sign in. He was standing in the main office area, in shackles. He had a chain around his waist, connected to two hand cuffs, and another chain leading to his feet, which was connected to ankle cuffs. I had seen this before on other inmates. It meant that George had committed a serious infraction and was being sent to Juvenile Hall in Santa Ana to go before a judge for additional punishment.

George and I were less than six feet apart, looking at each other, but neither of us spoke. I vowed to talk to George about this when I next saw him.

I didn't see him for another three months. When I asked his teacher about him, she said, "Oh! He's doing really well. He's not causing any trouble and is really studying."

George's PO also praised him, saying, "He's doing well. He doesn't get detention anymore. He's paid all of his restitution. In fact, I'm going to recommend that he come off probation."

When I asked George about his remarkable transformation, he simply told me, "I got tired of always being in trouble."

I suspect that George had developed respect for me and became ashamed when I saw in shackles. It made him think and led to his transformation. I worked with many probation clients, both adults and juveniles. I saw some improvement in many of the clients, but George is the only one who made such a remarkable turnaround.

I never saw George again, but I did see his PO several times and always asked about George. His reply: "No news is good news."

John Kirby, Chicago native, graduated from the U of I with a PhD in Aeronautical Engineering. After retiring from Boeing in California, he returned home. His interest in writing was engendered and encouraged by his first office mate, an editor of technical documents. John became an oddity within the engineering world, an engineer who liked to write reports. He found the Budlong Woods writers' group just four blocks from where he grew up and started attending so he could improve his writing skills. The works contained herein are his first published pieces.

My Favorite Things

Katherine Pappadimas

Red Wings

When I was 10 years old, my mother gave me a porcelain cardinal ring box. The bird was very delicate, posing with its wings spread. The wings reminded me of a miniature eagle. Its body was smaller than its wing span.

The cardinal is the Illinois State Bird. Its beauty is in its red color and wing span. Cardinals are special because they don't come out all the time. Once in a while you see them pose in a yard with snow on trees and bushes. In the springtime it seems that the cardinal waits to see me to sing his special song. He sits on a wire in the alley when I throw the garbage out. It never fails. Whether I live southwest or northwest, he sings, "I am here. I see you. Look up." When I look up and smile at him, he flies away.

When I sit in the yard in the summer, he sits on a fence not too far from me and sings, "I am here. I see you. Look at me!" I then smile at him and he flies away. I have my cardinal on my shelf and always take him with me. I can look back to spring, summer, and winter on the days the cardinal really sang and sings to me, "I am here. I see you. Look up." My cardinal won't go anywhere. He's mine.

Tiny Tears

One of my prized possessions is a Tiny Tears doll called Susan. I named her after my cousin. Her hair is very tightly curly and red. Her face is porcelain. Her cheeks are a rosy red that matches her lips. Her lips have a hole in the middle so I could feed her. She came with her own diaper bag, diapers, and a bottle. I also used to dress her.

I also had a baby brother, and when he turned three years old, he grabbed my Susan and threw her down the stairs. He was jealous of my doll! I cried and cried. Her cheek was scratched, and I wanted to take her to the doll hospital. The doctor at the doll hospital said, "If we leave the scratch, she will look more real." So for the rest of Susan's life, she had a scar on her porcelain cheek. My Susan is still with me.

My Golden Heart

Another favorite thing I own is an "I love you" heart. On our fifth anniversary my husband gave me a gold heart with one diamond in the middle. It was one ounce of gold. A heart is a way of saying "I love you." I don't like to take it off. Wouldn't it be nice if everyone had an "I love you" heart?

I am afraid to lose it. Right now I have too many people coming in and out of my house. So when I went to California, I gave the heart to my sister to hold so I don't lose it. She keeps jewelry in a safe deposit box. Now I feel better knowing it is safe with my sister.

Katherine Pappadimas is a very happy, retired teacher/librarian from the Chicago Public Schools. Katherine writes once in a while as the mood hits her. She enjoys the Budlong Woods group experience. She dreams of traveling and lucky numbers.

Photo by Carol Beu

A Fractured Fairy Tale

Vickie Scescke

One Sunday, as people milled around in the park after an Ella Jenkins concert, I ran into my friend Suzanne. We hadn't seen each other for awhile.

"How are you?" she asked. "What have you been doing?"

I started telling her about an interesting exhibit I had seen of bone chairs at the Karl Hammer gallery.

"Wait a minute. What did you say?" She reached into the loose, flowing folds of her long skirt and pulled out a pocket-sized notebook. The pocket from which she whipped the notebook was well hidden by generous fabric. "What gallery?" she asked.

It was a nice afternoon, so we stayed in the park and talked for a while. We talked about places, books, and food. Throughout the conversation she took notes. I had never seen this done before. It took me by surprise, but it wasn't really out of character. I knew Suzanne was quite an eccentric.

I recalled a day when we went for a drive. As always, she had her camera with her. She asked me to pull over now and then when something caught her eye, like an arrangement of plastic flowers in a windowsill (she loved kitsch) or a pile of metallic junk and old tires in a side yard.

"Stop!" she shouted abruptly as we went trolling through Pilsen in my rusted-out burgundy Olds.

"Where?" I asked, looking around for something of visual interest.

"Right here!" she said. I pulled over. She hopped out, and, to my surprise, took a picture of my own car. My husband had stuck a khaki green army jacket in the largest rust hole, and, unbeknownst to me, a sleeve had popped out, giving everyone an upside down wave as we drove by. She must have caught the reflection in a store front window as we passed.

Suzanne played with her pictures, juxtaposing them into a collage-like slide show. This was her art. I dabbled in collections, but Suzanne was a master collector. One year in a brochure for an art therapy conference, I saw that, in addition to the oral presentations, there would be a stall for trading visually intriguing stuff. Suzanne was the facilitator. As an art therapy student, I was required to go to the conference. What better way to skip a bunch of boring lectures yet still get credit for being there?

I scoured through my collections. I had stuffed my entire allotted storage space with cardboard, the broken down remains of large appliance boxes. I would be taking the el downtown to the conference, so this yielded nothing with trading potential. Realizing the need for portable items, I scanned my collection of cow, turkey, and chicken bones and selected a few. After snatching up some feathers, shells, and stones, I headed downtown.

Suzanne had bin after bin of miscellany: beads, buttons, scraps of fabric, bits of film, and numerous small machine parts, many that I cannot name. I parlayed my treasures into some miniature license plates measuring a half inch by an inch and various miniature cogs, springs, gaskets, and gears. I hung out with Suzanne for a while afterwards to watch what others brought and what they selected on the commodity exchange.

During trade lapses, I learned that Suzanne went to a weekly group for women interested in art and art therapy. She invited me to go and I went. That's how I met my friend Mary. She was the group leader. To a greater or lesser extent, we were a group of women piqued by found object and outsider art. We recognized the value of both for reclaiming lost or discarded parts of ourselves and society. We tried to emulate this art.

When I started going to Mary's group on the regular, I was pregnant with my second child. As the time for giving birth neared, the group decided to have a shower for me. But it was not your typical baby shower. The gifts given represented blessings, much like the blessings the fairy godmothers gave in Sleeping Beauty. Some of the gifts were handmade, and others were not. Mary gave a monkey puppet representing good humor. Suzanne gave a standing wooden puzzle of a bird and flower representing the gifts of music and beauty. Another member made a little Sculpey sculpture of a saucer with a naked girl and boy perched on its lip. Fate, a woman, one hand covering her eyes, the other pointing at the girl, stood in the middle of the saucer, foretelling the baby's sex. Another woman made a dream catcher to show the baby as a dreamer and visionary. A fifth member did not come. She was childless but very much wanted a baby. Perhaps she was jealous. She contended that it was wrong that all the attention was centered on one person. But, at least she did not put a curse on the baby.

Many of these blessings materialized. Fate got the sex right, and my daughter is a music lover and has always liked to dance. She cannot foretell the future like a visionary, but she also is not tethered by typical middle class biases. At three months, everyone said she looked like a baby orangutan. At three years, I hung a picture of her with her arms above her head, hands clasped, side by side with a postcard of a monkey in the exact same pose.

I always thought I would get a small hanging curio cabinet to put the objects in, but I never did. As my daughter grew, from time to time, I'd pull out these gifts and show them to her. The monkey hung in her room and she played with it. She would slip her hand in him, wrap his long arms around her neck, clasp his Velcro hands together, and sing to him, and they would dance, his feet dragging along the wooden floor of her room. The other gifts were wrapped in tissue paper and kept in a large shoe box. Some had writings that went with them. From time to time, we would carefully unwrap them, study them, read the writings, then rewrap them and place them back in their box.

The last time we got them out, my daughter was twenty-five and had her own apartment. The genitalia of the Sculpey boy had fallen off, but perhaps this was fitting.

"Would you like to take them to your place, or maybe let them go?"

"I don't know, Mom. I think not," she said as she turned one over in her hands, holding it delicately. "No, I am not going to fool around with blessings from fairy godmothers. It might evoke a curse."

"I agree," I said, breathing a sigh of relief. No hocus pocus. So we rewrapped them. Back in their shoe box they went. Then we packed them into the trunk where they are stored with other memorabilia, to be revisited in another five to ten years.

Original Artwork by Daniel Cleary

The Dark Forest Queen

Vickie Scescke

It is Michael, one of my myriad doubles partners, who first labels me The Double Fault Queen. I have played tennis for 14 years, and serving has always been my nemesis.

The form is hard to learn. I hire a coach early on. "Pronate, then snap the wrist," he tells me.

Pronate? What does that even mean? I go home and look it up in my well-worn dictionary, a Collins New World Dictionary of the American Language, Second College Edition. Its spine is held together with packing tape and certain pages are missing. Pronate, on the page beginning with prologuize and ending with proneness, is still there. "To rotate (the hand or forearm) so that the palm faces down or towards the body," I read. Hmm, wouldn't that happen after you snap your wrist? "From the Latin, pronare," my beloved dictionary tells me. I think he means the opposite. What is the opposite of pronate? Supinate, I suppose. I look it up just to be sure. But what does it matter? Knowing the words doesn't mean I can execute a good serve.

Despite the coaching, serving remains difficult over the ensuing years. At first it seems mostly a matter of finding the box. The service box is actually rather large, 283.5 square feet to be exact. Seems like that would be easy enough to hit, no? The challenge soon metamorphoses into the ball toss. The ball develops an incredibly fast spin, making it hard to focus on. I try different ways of holding the ball to eliminate the spin: fingertips, palm of the hand, like a coffee cup between thumb and index finger, to no avail. My teammate looks back at me. "Just hit it in," she invariably says. What do you think I'm trying to do? I want to scream. But I don't say anything, alone in my struggle. Until one day I do.

"You double fault too much," one teammate says when I am having a particularly bad day.

I have endured discussions of toss, position of the hand, elbow and feet, arch of the back, etcetera and etcetera. It all just makes me more up in my head. And now this. You double fault too much? Isn't that just stating the obvious? I say loudly that I am not going to talk about it anymore. "Don't even say the words in my presence," I say. "Anyone who wants to talk about it, well, go find someone else to talk to, because I will turn my back and walk away." I turn my back and walk away.

I don't stop thinking about it though. I invent euphemisms for it. Whenever D F comes to mind I substitute
dark forest,
deep fissure,
dank foundation,
anything but

that dreaded phrase.
I amuse myself in this way, although,
these words too are negative.
why not
delicate finger foods
cut like dainty flowers
during forenoons of
delicious fornication
spent dipping fondues?

If I can do these mental gymnastics, why can't I just serve the ball? The mystery
is that sometimes things go well. I float the ball up to the perfect point and hit it,
no problem, good focus, good body control, with no thought of how I am holding
the ball or moment of release; natural, like breathing. These good times can go on
for months. But sooner or later, like a camera lens slipping out of focus, things go
haywire.

The ball seems to sprout wings and fly from side to side, even behind my back, flit-
ting here and there like a bird. Sometimes I run after it and try to hit it. Other times
I let it drop. Sometimes it goes up in the air and heads back down into my face,

growing chicken claws as it falls,
pinkish yellow and scaly,
diving straight for my nose.
I try to swat it with my racket
or shield my face with my arms.
    How can I talk about these things with my tennis friends?
    Would they ever understand?
    Oh, sure, they occasionally deep fissure,
    but not like me,
    no, nothing like me,
    I am the Dark Forest Queen.
    But just the same
    I'm still in the game.

Photo by Robynne Wallace

104

Waiting Room, January 16, 2018

Vickie Scescke

The waiting seems interminable. To think about something other than what she awaits, Bridget eavesdrops, picking up snatches from conversations of others who also are waiting.

"They say thar ain't a thang wrong with him."

"Same day I buried my cousin, you know what I mean. I knowed him all my life."

This is the twang of her childhood, and it lulls her, easing her anxiety. It's the vision she fears, not so much what she'll hear. At least the waiting room is visually appealing, windows from floor to ceiling on one side, looking out on the streets of Lexington, finally cleared of Monday's snow. The sun is peaking out; a single hawk or crow flies in the sky. Smoke spews from the chimney of the house across the street, blooming in the cold air.

The sight of it she fears, she dreads, tubes running in and out of orifices and newly gouged holes, lights blinking, eyes closed, a hunk of pale, pink, swollen flesh lying in the bed.

The sitting and waiting...don't think, just don't think. More snippets of conversation come to her ears from the left and the right. She weaves them together into a tapestry of words to bolster her up.

"The whole dam bunch... he said he's as old as I am, just about, damn near sixty-seven."

"Lef him in thar?"

"Lef him in thar," echoed, intonation rising at the end for emphasis, almost like a question.
"Ever Tuesday, I get my Reese's cup at Dairy Queen, ever Tuesday"

"If you's over at Dairy Queen, you'd pay seven dollars fer it. You go over thar, and you git yerself a little ole sundae, and you pay seven or eight dollars fer it.",,,

Bridget had arrived in Lexington from Louisville the day before via Uber—longest ride he had ever given a client, the young driver had told her. She'd allowed her license to expire, so they wouldn't rent her a car at the airport.

"Three days, my license is only three days past the expiration date. Isn't there a one-week grace period?" she argued with the agent at the counter.

"State law, ma'am," he replied tersely.

There was very little traffic on the road because of the snow. They passed a mail truck off the road in the ditch. It was beautiful, the ride, horse and cattle farms covered in snow. The driver was chatty, and Bridget relaxed in the back seat. Well worth the one hundred dollars she thought; she didn't have to drive the seventy odd miles in the snow.

Bridget's cell phone dings. It's her brother looking for some kind of answer. "Nothing yet," she replies, "still waiting."

She was almost proud when she walked into her mother's room the night before. Her mom was up on one elbow, nude, wild-eyed, disconnecting suction cups attached to her chest, and as Bridget approached the bed, she disconnected the last cup with its tube still attached and gave it a fling. It hit the footboard with a metallic clang.

"Hello, Bridget" her mother said, as if she had been doing something normal, like frying up some eggs. There was no feeding tube, no collar to protect her broken neck, no IV, nothing referred to in the myriad phone calls from nurses and hospital personnel in the past week. She began to swing her legs over the side of the bed, as if she was going to get up.

A nurse rushed in.

"Sorry you had to see your mom like that," she apologized. She went on to explain that the cups and tubes were necessary to monitor her. She put her hospital gown and neck brace back on efficiently while talking.

"But what about the feeding tube?" Bridget asked. "I got a call Saturday telling me that a feeding tube was going to be inserted in her nose."

"She had that torn out by the next morning."

She looked at her mom's nose. Thank God there were no visible bloody scars.

Relieved, Bridget almost snorted. Her mom was fighting, fighting to regain some control, fighting not to be drugged up, tied down, monitored, all the dehumanizing things that happen in hospitals in the name of health.

"Has she had anything to eat?" Bridget knew her mom had been there for six days already.
"Whatever she had on Saturday through the tube," the nurse responded. She went on to reiterate what Bridget had already heard on the phone, that her mom had failed her swallowing test, that she could aspirate and die with any intake of food, even pureed.

The buzzer goes off on the table by the chair where Bridget is sitting, bringing her out of her reverie. Time to see how the surgery went, she thinks as she rises and walks to the desk. You can do this, she tells herself. At least, for now, the waiting is over.

Photo by Carol Beu

The Ides of March, 2019

Vickie Scescke

Significant
then not so much
Relatively so
until proven irrelevant.

Who mourns the passing of the seedlings not yet emerged from the soil?
But the seed cultivator who let the trays all dry out
Too tired
preferring two beers and let's see what's on TV
The next day he dissects a pot
And finds the little yellow-brown dead thing
Its future first two leaves folded like tiny hands in prayer.

Baby killer
        he mutters to himself.

Beneath the surface
An oval-shaped tumorous egg forms, grows
Cut it out!
says the man with the stethoscope necklace
And in doing so he nicks the colon
The body dies of sepsis within the week.

March days march on
The gray sky kneels down to the dirty pavement
And the remaining filthy fragments of gritty snow
Testify while they can.

Is it really all that bad?
The teacher asks the sullen-eyed girl
sitting in the not-quite-back of the class
She draws great maps
But they spark no interest in travel.

In the beginning was the word
She reads
That failed to fill the void of silence within her.

A sparkling star in the night sky
Marks one finite point in the vastness of time and space
It is the Ides of March.

What **Vickie Scescke** writes about next is a mystery, memoir inspired or imaginative thought; she runs the gamut. Like a tennis ball bouncing through the genres, or a Jack/Jane in the box, likes a pleasant surprise, her writing popping out of the box.

Photo by Carol Beu

The Perfect Meal

Judy SooHoo

As Child
Surrounded with loud cheers and laughter of friends. The clacking of mahjong tiles long into New Year's Day. My father's masterful, velvety, tasty feast for the eyes and tummies. "Fat Man's" opening of bottled pop with large pudgy hands amid a crowd of squealing children who followed whispering and hushed into the kitchen each and every time. The cool scent of fresh evergreen fir lit with big bold-colored, teardrop-shaped bulbs perfectly reflected in the backdrop of fluffy white snowflakes hung swirling in air.

Married
Three home-cooked dishes each week night. I with my mainstay of the perfect holy trinity of chicken, ham and Chinese sausage, stir-fried rice noodles, and seasoned shrimp. Hours-long lasagna on weekends. He with his "world-famous" meatloaf, juicy sweet spareribs or day-long cooked burgundy onions. Leftovers tucked away for the next day. Dishes washed together in a big sinkfull of soapy water. Tea for two to finish off the night.

As Single Parent
One dish for dinner, shared. A wide palate from adult food to fast food. Perfect in the car between this class and that.

With Friends
Rounds and rounds of "Where do you want to go?" and "I don't care" end in a stand-out charitable enterprise, free pie Wednesdays, a Swedish standby, late night Chinese or a 24/7 Mexican or urban diner. A time full of tear-filled laughter, thoughtful opinions, searing witticisms, reminiscences of triumphs and mistakes, quiet reveals, life's highlights in a perfect slice.

As Caregiver
Home-cooked dishes guided by the food pyramid. The perfect-sized meal, a Costco Australian rack of lamb. Eight little loins, two each, a curved bone with crusty fat gripped firmly. Tender enough for chewing, accompanied by greens, sometimes clear-broth, winter melon or watercress soup. Sweet potato or rice for a starch.

Alone
A large, juicy, red strawberry or two. Fat blueberries by the handful or a firm ripe banana balancing on newly discovered cereal, perfectly-packed with protein, vitamins and fiber sitting in lactose-free, vanilla-flavored almond milk.

I Am From

Judy SooHoo

I am from joy as a girl born in America, the "Golden Mountain," the land of hopes and dreams— giving the family the fancied one son/one daughter, coveted as much as a male

I am from a working class neighborhood of third-floor walk-ups lined up buddy-buddy, a corner store that sold penny candy, a corner drug store and other stores you could walk to, a community of familiar families and faces flowing with hard-earned cash and living the good life in the present but also saving S&H green stamps from the A&P and small bills for money-filled Chinese red envelopes for children and the elderly

I am from St. Therese on Chicago's south side Chinatown taught by Maryknoll missionary sisters, from typical clothes, except for the day I refused to go to school in the new sailor outfit complete with a rectangular flap, a target across my back; from St. Ita on the north side, one of two Asians in the school, and from the annual trek for green plaid jumpers with white blouses on Clark Street

I am from tag in street shadows to outrun the heat of the night, hopscotch, jump rope, and boys playing marbles with aggies, cats' eyes, and shooters

I am from a rare day off to Grant Park, Buckingham Fountain, window-shopping at Marshall Field's, Baskin's, Lytton's, and a one-pound treat of Woolworth's freshly sliced baked ham while glancing longingly at the huge soda fountain

I am from my father's cold, crisp smell of winter wool carrying a daily newspaper underarm and Saturday morning walks with his little girl to the local coffee shop— an enclave for men—for my orange soda pop

I am from Christmas merriment, good food, good cheer, and the clickety-clack of mahjong tiles ringing in the New Year with hundreds of ear-popping firecrackers clearing the way for the colorful and scary wide-mouth lion, dancing and spreading good fortune throughout

I am from surprise toys from Cracker Jack and Boton rice candy with an inner rice paper wrapper you never knew was really edible; kitchen play sets, paper dolls, and Barbie and Ken in a pink vinyl carrying case filled with clothes my mother sewed

I am from spell-binding, mercury-based pellets of Magic Snakes lit by my brother, baseball in the living room with the front curtains drawn taut, a broken bed frame, from playing "trampoline," a cold, wet mattress from a burst water balloon and getting caught sneaking out the back door when returning through the front—a lesson need only learned once

I am from excruciatingly hours-long wedding banquets of 12 courses with the much-anticipated last dishes of long-life noodles and special fried rice and then the mad rush to exit with leftovers in Chinese carry-out boxes and unfinished bottles of Hennessy, Johnnie Walker, or a liter of pop in prized hands

I am from treats of Ovaltine mornings, Borden's Sweetened Condensed Milk, and Sunday- and black tea-only dim sum presented in rolling steam carts, TV dinners on TV trays in front of the black and white tube TV, and my father's cooking, otherwise, steamed Chinese sausage with rice, Campbell's Condensed Cream of Mushroom Soup, or other conveniences like canned pink salmon over a bed of lettuce flash-cooked with seasoned oil

I am from Saturday morning cartoons, Tom and Jerry, Rocky and Friends, Fred Flintstone, The Jetsons, and The Three Stooges; The Bozo Show at noon; The Wonderful World of Disney Sunday evenings; Dark Shadows rushing home after school

I am from Senn High School, an integrated public high school with lockdowns and locker checks for weapons

I am from Nancy Drew, the Hardy Boys, Archie Comics, Betty and Veronica, and newspaper cartoons Peanuts, Sylvia, Doonesbury, and Dilbert

I am from 8-track reel-to-reel tapes of Chinese opera blaring and clanging on Saturday mornings, LPs of the whistling and crackling soundtrack to A Fistful of Dollars and Blowing in the Wind, Leaving on a Jet Plane, Bridge Over Troubled Water, Cats in the Cradle, American Bandstand, and the Beatles

I am from an immigrant family starting without language or skills laboring in sewing factories, hand laundries, and 365-days-a-year restaurants and me ironing shirts, folding socks, pressing clothes, waiting on tables, tending bar, cashiering, hosting, and, when crazy busy, in the kitchen making fried rice and egg foo young—in proudly owned family businesses

I am from cultures oceans apart—of thoughts and deeds worlds divided yet merged into one

I am from past secrets never to be known and a future to be explored

For Marty

Judy SooHoo

Hopes
Our could have beens, our should have beens

Dreams
What we dared, unfettered

Life
Our wants, our gets
Tears, fears
No regrets, life
Lived

Truth
What we seek, what matters

Love
Ever kindling, never ending

Photo by Carol Beu

Profile in Black

Judy SooHoo

37 stops
16 shots score the goal
Laquan McDonald
41 shots attempted by four
Amadou Diallo
12 shots for penalties
Michael Brown

37 stops
1 shot for a shoot-out until sudden death
Trayvon Martin
1 plastic bag over head for rain delay
Sandra Bland
50+ baton twirls in the air
Rodney King

37 stops
Chokehold wins the takedown
Eric Garner
Spinal cord injury ends the game
Freddie Gray
Mother and child scream from behind the paint
Philando Castile

37 stops
Out of bound plays stop the clock but not the game
Balls fly and pucks whiz through the air
Deep into the crowd
37 stops too many

Note: 37 stops is one black man's account of how many times he has been racially profiled and stopped by police.

Judy SooHoo is relatively new to writing, having started with personal essays. Thanks to the expertise and support of the Budlong Woods Writers, she has started to explore poetry writing as a second effective form for creative expression and is quite adroit at evoking emotional response in whatever form she attempts.

Ode to My Sweet

A. Sylvan

True love is a rocky road
but you never forget your first real passion
It was DarkChocolateNuts&SeaSalt
A most satisfying treat
We got on for years

Alas, temptation reared its head
Faithful at the candy counter takes real character
I strayed
But not so far, only to DarkChocolateMochaAlmond
My bond with chocolate was solid, enduring

Then the ultimate betrayal
I spurned chocolate and declared allegiance to CaramelAlmond&SeaSalt

Heartless, I went on to have a cocoa-free dalliance with CrunchyPeanutButter
Followed by the briefest of interludes with MapleGlazedPecan&SeaSalt

But the estrangement could not last
Chocolates charms slowly, inevitably drew me back
The tender DarkChocolateCherryCashew would not be ignored
We've been an item for weeks now
I think this is going to last

Anne Sylvan was born in Chicago. She left for 15 years and happily returned. She writes about creatures, human and otherwise, along with places and things. Anne came to poetry only two years ago and is glad she did.

Photo by Enid Fefer

My Mother 2

Helen Um

My mother came to America in December in 1981. I was her only living child. I had came to America with my three children to study nursing at Indiana Nursing College in April of that year. My husband stayed in Korea to finish a Master of Divinity course joining us in America a year later in May. My mother supported us by babysitting while my husband helped in the Korean church. Our whole family moved to Chicago from Indiana in April 1985.

God inspired me to start the Comprehensive Korean Self-Help Center on October 12, 1985. We received a grant from the New York Presbytery Self-Help. October 12th is the same date Columbus arrived in America. My mother helped poor and needy people by providing information on job opportunities. She still babysat and gave her income to help new immigrants. She worked as a Korean community health worker at the center. After office hours, she answered the telephone.

They had bilingual community health workers at the center.

Late on a cold day, a client came to the center to enroll in the energy program. The bilingual community health worker told the client in English, "Come tomorrow."

My mom had recognized the English word "tomorrow" and asked the worker in Korean, "Why did you tell the client to come tomorrow on this cold day?" The client was taken care of that day because of my mother.

There were homeless people who stayed at the center. My mother liked to cook food for all and would help those who slept there. She was a devoted woman. She would not come home to rest, instead staying with them at the center.

I would like to tell you about the center's program. There were many immigrants and poor people with several needs.

- We provided a food pantry program for over 1000 people. There were about 30-40 volunteers for the food distribution program, and my mom prepared lunch for all of them.
- The center had health programs for the uninsured who sought help from dentists and medical and eye doctors.
- We provided counseling programs for any and all disturbed people.
- A legal counseling program was available for undocumented people.
- We provided nine English classes for the adults and seven children's after school programs.
- We had a bulletin board to inform people of job opportunities.
- We had a weekly prayer group.
- We had many volunteers, and we had to train them.
- We had fundraising programs, such as garage sales.

We are proud of the programs. My mother was involved in almost all of them.

She is still concerned for needy people. She prays for the sick people around her, and she cooks food for any sick people in her apartment building. Just recently my mother turned 100 years old in Korean age. In Korea the first birthday is the day you are born. She eats very well, and she can cook food, do laundry, clean her room, and take a bath by herself. I am very thankful for my mother's health. I have prayer time with her every morning and evening. My mother still recalls hymns and bible verses. I go to church with her every Sunday.

* * *

We celebrated my mother's birthday in her building, the Schneider apartments, and had another party at the church after worship. My mom has six great grandchildren. They prepared food and had a musical program to celebrate her as some of them can play the violin, guitar, cello, and piano.

My mom's perception of a party was not the same as ours. She thinks that she has to feed hungry people. I was very thankful for my mother's 100th birthday party, but my mom said, "Why do you like to have a party? Everybody can eat food. Why do you like to take other people's time? It is burden on them."

My mother has two daughters, but one is in heaven. I have three children, and my sister has two children. My son's family members live in LA, and my daughter's family members are in Peoria. My other son's family lives in Chicago. My niece and nephew live in Chicago. My husband is in Korea, and he is busy with his ministry work, so he was not able to participate in the celebrations. I was sorry that we could not be together for our 57th wedding anniversary on April 23rd. Although he is busy with his work, he still sends money and clothes and provides emotional support over the phone.

My mother wore a white dress on Easter Sunday. She looked very nice. She loves to go to church. She got up early, ate breakfast, put on makeup, and put on her special dress. The church bus came to pick up my mom, and it took one hour to get to church. On the bus church members shared their life stories and sang hymns. Mom enjoyed meeting church members and ask hearing about their life stories in the last week. She also loved hearing the Easter Cantata choir and the sermons, which were about Jesus's resurrection. Jesus died for our sin, and God raised him from dead. This occasion is the best event for Christians. My mom really liked to hear this. Isn't that wonderful news about resurrection? After worship the church provided a very nice Korean dinner with fried beef, pork, spinach, salad, fruits, and rice with special colorful eggs wrapped with white cloths.

* * *

My mother was in good health for her 100th birthday party, but a little while after that she fell down in the hall while trying to pick up a small piece of trash. I called 911, and she was taken to the hospital. She could not breathe because of the severe pain. The doctor in the emergency room prescribed pain medication. The following day she had surgery to treat a hip fracture. Before the surgery, the doctor was concerned about her heart because she is 100 years old. The heart doctor checked her heart and said she could have the surgery, which was a success. She stayed at Swedish Covenant Hospital for five days and was then transferred to Fairmont Nursing home. She stayed at the nursing home for a month and half.

She came home and she was able to walk with a walker. When my mom told me that she had fallen while trying to pick up trash in the hall, I cried, "Why did you try to pick it up? Why?" After that we had evening devotion. We read the bible story about Joseph (Genesis 45:1-15). When Joseph could no longer control himself before all his attendants, he cried out he wept so loudly that the Egyptians heard. Joseph said to his brothers, "I am Joseph. Is my father still living? It was not you who sent me here, but God. God sent me here ahead of you to save our families." Joseph met his brothers after 13 years. He did not ask them "Why did you sell me here?" but I asked my mom why she tried to pick up the trash. After three months of suffering, I was very upset. After that I cried and repented. I would like to learn from Joseph's faith in God.

* * *

My mother is walking with a walker again, but I have to follow her with the wheelchair in case she gets tired. Usually, she does her foot and hand exercise before she starts walking. She sees a physical therapist twice in a week. He told me that she is one of his clients who follows instructions best. She is eating and sleeping well. She takes pain medication every two or three days and goes to the church every Sunday to meet God and her grandchildren. It takes her six hours to go to the church and come back, but she never gets tired. She believes that God cured her sickness during worship time at the church. She comes to exercise class every morning, and afterward, we holds hands together and pray. Somebody said prayer works, and my mom is a witness to that. I really appreciated God's help and people's help. She has a housekeeper five days per week. She watches Christian TV to hear sermons. Her health is improving. When she was very sick, my children helped, remembering how she was there for them. They raised her bed up and bought side rails for it. They brought food and clothes. I much appreciated my children's help.

Last week when my mom was using her walker, with me keeping her company, we met one of the residents in the Schneider apartments who used to walk but was now pushing himself in a wheelchair, having had his left leg amputated. My mom was shocked. He told us that he'd had a blood clot problem that caused gangrene of the foot. The doctor decided to amputate the left leg below the knee.

We met him again as he was pushing himself in the wheelchair into the dining room. He told me that he used to smoke cigarettes a lot, which led to a disease that caused his foot to have gangrene and that he will need an artificial leg—then he will be able to dance again. Even though he was talking positively, I could tell he was depressed.

I called my son and told him about the man's problem. I asked my son to cut down on his smoking. My son told me that he was quitting smoking but that it is very hard. I realized that quitting would be a very important factor in maintaining a healthy life. At no point during her life did my mom smoke, drink, or take drugs, and she has lived 100 years. She eats small portions of food that are low in fat, salt, and sugar, and she walks frequently. She likes to read the bible and sing hymns. Once you develop a habit, it is hard to change, so it is helpful to learn coping mechanisms such as talking to family members and friends, spiritual care (meditation), and positive thinking (1 Thessalonians 5:16-18).

* * *

The other week, my mom was watching TV and heard about North Korea's problems with the United States and its neighbors. She has good eyesight and hearing, so she understands. She was very worried about war. I told her about how historian John Keegan wrote, "The first world war was a tragic and unnecessary conflict."

She remembered the Korean War too, and how many people were killed and wounded. Many people lost families and experienced poverty. She said, "We don't need war. We need peace. How can we solve this problem? We need God's help, so we have to pray for North Korea. There are many people starving to death and suffering due to human rights issues." We wonder who is helping North Korea develop missiles. Kim Jong-un is too young to lead a country. We cannot trust North Korea. There have been three generations of leaders acting like they are God. North Korean people cannot complain about problems. If they do, they die or suffer even more. So people try to leave North Korea, but if they caught they die or receive harsh punishment. God help us to help North Korean people.

October 4th was Korean Thanksgiving day, which we call Chu Seuuk. We had a party at the Schneider apartment building. We bought food from the Korean grocery store, and we made Korean pancakes, cooked fish, soup, kimchi and, rice; and we bought rice cakes (song pyun) and oranges. First we had a simple devotion and then dinner.

My mom is very thankful for everything we have. She is always thankful in any situation, even when she faces problems. In the bible Paul said, "My grace is sufficient for you, for my power is made perfect in weakness. Therefore, I will boast all the more gladly about my weaknesses, so that Christ's power may rest on me. That is why, for Christ's sake, I delight in weaknesses, in insults, in hardships, in persecutions, in difficulties. For when I am weak, then I am strong." My mom loves these bible verses because even though she is weaker than before, but she is strong in Christ. She always says that we have to learn to give thanks to God in any situation (2 Corinthians 12:8-10).

* * *

I am my mom's only living daughter and a special nurse. Therefore, I am very concerned about her health. She complains about more pain at her operation site, and she cannot walk with a walker like before. She needs more frequent medication to relieve her pain. What is the reason for this pain? I would like to find out. When we went to church, it took us about six hours to go and return home. Maybe that trip caused more pain. My mom has to get up to void almost every hour during the night time, so that might contribute to her pain. Her physical therapy was discontinued, but she might need another physical therapist. I do what I can.

My daughter told me that she was worried about her grandma and her mom and prayed about the problem. During prayer time, she saw vision of diaper pad, and she called me and told me she was sending diaper pads so Grandma won't have to get up during the night. It is amazing that it is helping a lot. It is the grace of God during Thanksgiving season.

My mom is eating OK but has smaller amounts of food and more frequently. Her bodily functions are OK. Sometimes she asks the same question over again. We have devotion together for spiritual support. She does some tasks on her own because I am here to help her. I believe that is why she is doing so great. If she goes to a nursing home, her condition will decline without family support. I pray that she will be able walk like before.

* * *

While I was in the washroom, I heard bang sound, and I ran to my mom's room and found that she had fallen off of the bed. I asked my friend for a ride to the Swedish Covenant Hospital emergency room. They took x-rays of the right side of her head, shoulder, lower back, and leg. There was no fracture, but she had a brain hemorrhage, so she went to the intensive care unit. They did not give me permission to stay, so I went home around midnight. I returned to the ICU in the morning, and my mom told me she was scared that she was alone. The neurosurgeon said that the hemorrhage area is small, so she was moved out of the ICU to the regular floor. She was a little bit confused because of the hemorrhage. She was acting very strange and irritable and shouting. She did not recognize me, so I was scared and I told her that I was going home. She became very upset, so I stayed and the nurse gave me a bed. I felt guilty that I told her I would go home. I prayed to God to forgive me, and I called my husband and cried. I should not have told her that. She was scared to be in the American Hospital where no one spoke Korean.

She stayed in the hospital for six days and then she came home, and she relaxed here. She is eating and sleeping well again. If she has a helper, she can walk with the walker, and is able to take a shower. I really thank God. She is OK.

Helen Um is a special nurse to her mother of 100 years. Anyone who has done any caregiving knows how hard this can be, but Helen does not complain. She finds her strength in God and his son, Jesus Christ. Helen shares her struggles and looks for solutions, finding them in prayer.

Accolades for "Cows on Parade"
A tribute to the outdoor exhibition displayed throughout Chicago in 1999

Robynne Wallace

One summer, I went touring, though I never left my town.
Still, I felt like a tourist with the cows placed all around.
I found it quite refreshing that a city bus or two
Could take me to a part of town that suddenly seemed new.

Our friendly town seemed friendlier; the people on the street
Spoke freely to each other on the meaning of the fleet.
They asked for cow locations, talked of places they had dined,
And stopped to photograph their kids with cows of every kind.

They spoke of different cows they'd seen and easily had fun
Discussing all their fav'rites and exchanging bovine puns.
These people came from everywhere—how nice to have the chance
To meet so many friendly folks who shared bovine romance.

Though I went "cowing" many times, alone or with my friends,
I also once brought 60 kids to learn artistic trends.
To those who said it wasn't art, I say, "You're full of hay!"
I'd rather stroll our cow-lined streets than browse the MCA!

Mo-sa-ics, textures, paint, collage all teach art education,
And some cows showed that flattery is shown by imitation
With three Picassos, one Monet, Chagall, Matisse, Miro;
A Pollock, Warhol, Mondrian, Leonardo, and van Gogh.

Since public art is art-for-all, the public art was free—
And cows provided 20 weeks of art for all to see.
And best—they gave exposure to the artists of our city.
It's strange that no one thought of this before—and such a pity.

This might have been a thought-out plan or just a stroke of luck,
But tourists spent a staggering two hundred million bucks!
And I'm quite sure that money got distributed around
To groups needing assistance in all corners of our town.

Though many had predicted that those cows would be a bust—
That herd stampeded negative predictions into dust.
When auctioned off for charity, the cows made three mil more,
Revealing to the skeptics just what Daley did it for.

Who'd think those cows could make a giant splash the way they did?
Who'd think that cows could make me once again feel like a kid?
Who'd think the cows could please the rich, the poor, the large and small?
Bob Green was right the day he wrote, "The cows have fooled us all!"

Previously published "Untitled" in the Lerner Newspaper, 2/24/2000

Robynne Wallace a writer since childhood was bitten by the photography bug in her late teens. Both have been a part of her life ever since. As an art teacher when "Accolates to Cows on Parade" was written, she accompanied dozens of tweens on a field trip so they could experience first hand the inner and outer beauty that she saw in the ceramic cows. Presently her photography and designwork are displayed at a local gallery, but her guilty pleasure will always be writing.

Photos by Robynne Wallace

The Little Mermaid Knows
(a Golden Shovel Poem)

Vivian J. Williford

This I truly, positively know: that only
until you have existed with her in the
depths of her bewitching under-sea world, little could you understand what the
mermaid
had to sacrifice for mortal love; she knows
her precious sweet golden voice, the
enchanting kingdom of beauty—what a price
for a mortal world, a mortal Prince; one
is seduced and can't foresee who pays
to say farewell forever, and what for?
mortal love, yes, mysterious mortal love;
wish her a happy ever after ending, what
we all dream of when making a lover's sacrifice.

"Only the little mermaid knows the price
 one pays for love, what sacrifice."
—From "The Little Mermaid"
by Anne Morrow Lindbergh
(After Hans Christian Anderson's story)

Photo by Carol Beu

My Mermaid Collection

Vivian J. Williford

Everyone keeps asking me, "Why mermaids?"

I can't really answer that for sure. Maybe there is a spiritual or deep soul connection of some sort? Maybe the mythological sirens have me under a spell? Maybe, as Shirley MacLaine might say, "I was a mermaid in a past life." Really, the reason I love mermaids has changed more than a few times over the years. What I can pinpoint exactly is discovering and acquiring my very first mermaid.

Let me start by recalling that, as an enchanted and bewildered young child, I loved hearing stories about mermaids and imagined swimming and living among them in the sea. I even had my imaginary friend, Goldie the mermaid, to play with. At that time I lived near the ocean and loved everything connected with it, except for maybe the scary sharks.

When I married and we were setting up our first little apartment, the decorations were all nautically themed. My husband Pete and I shared a love of the ocean. Our choice of decor really made us both comfortable. We enjoyed setting up a few fish tanks and collected some lovely tropical fish. We also had some beautiful collectible sea shells and other nautical decorations scattered around the apartment.

In 1955, Pete and I were living in Brooklyn, New York. One day I was walking alone down Flatbush Avenue just taking care of business when I spied an incredible mermaid in the window of a little gift shop. She was an all black clay sculptured vase with a simple design that was so appealing. I just knew at first sight that she would be coming home with me. The mermaid stood about a foot high, and even though she was designed to be a vase she didn't need any flowers displayed in her to look lovely. There I stood on the sidewalk staring at her, thinking how perfect she would look standing next to our beautiful fish tanks.

My budget for knick-knack stuff at that time was non-existent, but I could not have cared less. I had to have this irresistible mermaid that seemed to be luring me to take her home. So I just marched into the shop to find out the price and get a closer look at her. She had been made in Mexico and even signed by the artist. Even though it was an impulsive and very unnecessary purchase, I just bought her with some of that week's grocery money.

I couldn't wait until Pete came home to see our new nautical treasure standing in all her glory next to the fish tanks on the room divider. He didn't quite share all of my enthusiasm for her, but at least he didn't make me take her back to the little shop. This first mermaid purchase over 60 years ago ended up starting the huge collection I have today.
This mermaid is now named "The Black Madonna." A dear old friend of mine,

Becky, insisted on naming her that when my collection started to really accumulate. Becky was a very spiritual-minded friend and felt that the Black Madonna was very special and that every women has somewhere in her home a Madonna. The Black Madonna is now surrounded by hundreds of other mermaids and mermen that decorate every room of my apartment. She started out as just a simple knick-knack, but she's now my mermaid queen. She is so precious to me that I always hand carried her each time I moved for fear that she would be broken or lost.

Who knows how some collections start or where they may end up? I just know I love living in my mythical mermaid world, and I like to share it with my family and friends. After all, they have certainly added to my collection many times with mermaid gifts for special occasions. Almost every mermaid on display has a story or a sweet, fond memory for me. These mermaids were not my first serious collection, but I can say absolutely, positively, without a shadow of a doubt, that they will be my last.

Long live the mermaids and the mermen too!

Photo by Katherine Pappadimas

The Golden Hour Clock

Vivian J. Williford

The Golden Hour Clock is a golden memory for me. Every few years or so, I think of doing a search and trying again to buy an old working Golden Hour Clock to live the rest of my life with—a bucket list kind of thing. I had this clock back in 1953 in my first apartment. My husband Pete and I bought it from a premiums catalog with Raleigh cigarette coupons. Back in those days almost everyone smoked and we smoked Raleigh cigarettes because they had these gift coupons. As newlyweds, we purchased lots of neat stuff for our apartment with both cigarette coupons and Green Stamp books.

Back to the clock, which I dearly loved. First of all, it was kind of like a puzzle to figure out how it worked. It looked like a round clear plate of glass with the hands moving, almost floating, from the pinpoint center as if by magic. The outside of the glass and the base were trimmed with gold. It was powered by an electric cord. That wonderful clock sat in my living rooms for over 40 years. Sadly, it stopped working one day, and I did take it to a clock repair shop. Unfortunately, I couldn't afford to bring it back to life at that time, and had to say farewell. There has never been another clock in my life that matched my fondness for my old Golden Hour one.

 One of the big reasons I fell in love with this special clock in the first place is what was printed on the box it came in. I will never forget it, and I regret I didn't save that part of the box. In big letters it said "ONLY COUNT THE GOLDEN HOURS." This has been one of my lifelong mantras that I try to remember. I would love to again have another Golden Hour clock to count the rest of my golden hours.

{Postscript}
The above story was written for my Tuesday morning writing class on August 9, 2016. After I read my piece, the teacher suggested that I should tell my family of my wish. I did just that, and I am so happy I did. On my 85th birthday, November 1, 2016, my son Paul presented me with a working Golden Hour Clock that he was able to track down. I was so excited when I saw it that I actually cried a bit. Wow—another bucket list desire I can scratch off the list. Wishes do come true. Thank you so very much, Paul. I love you and my new old clock. Now if it isn't pushing my luck too much, I wish to have lots more golden hours and years to enjoy it.

Feathers Feathers Everywhere

Vivian J. Williford

Feathers feathers everywhere
When you look you see
Feathers lying on the ground
The birds have set them free

Feathers decorate so many things
Oh thank you little bird
You've even heard of horse feathers
But that really is absurd

Have you seen feather dusters, feather masks, and a feathered hat? Feather pillows, feather comforters? And the one that's in your cap?

Then there are feathered angel wings
And vests filled with down
Also quill pens to write with
And now how does this sound?

Feathered nests and featherbedding
Feather stitching, a feather brain
Featherweights and feathered haircuts
Enough to drive a bird insane

Feathered boas and feather fans
Feathered arrows in the air
Think by now you get the message
Feathers feathers everywhere

Hoping that this little poem
Has really tickled you
Because that's another thing
A feather can really do

Goldie the Mermaid

Vivian J. Williford

> Twin tails on mermaids
> Wings on their sisters
> Fish tails that glitter
> No tootsies with blisters
> I'm going to tell you
> A tale of a tail
> This fable is from my life
> It begins in a pail

A long, long, time ago, when I was about four or five years young, my favorite place to be in the summertime was Jones Beach on Long Island. At that age I was not interested so much in swimming. What I really liked was being at the water's edge. My mommy always made me wear a little inflated inner tube over my bathing suit. What I loved was playing with my little beach pail and shovel. That pail was a gift from the Easter Bunny. It was originally filled with green paper grass, chocolate bunnies, and colorful jelly beans. The pail was so pretty, decorated with sea shells, mermaids, and my name in big blue letters.

I could play for hours all by myself at the water's edge building sandcastles. One day after I had built a beautiful castle, I decided to dig a moat around it and fill it with water. I took my pail to get water many times to try to fill up my moat. On my last weary trip from the water, I heard someone calling my name. I looked to my family sitting on the sand and enjoying the beach. No one was calling me. I heard my name again, but I still couldn't see anyone calling me.

I plopped down on the warm sand with my pail of water, and for the third time I heard my name being called. That time I could hear that I was being called from inside the pail. I looked down and could not believe what my little eyes saw. At first it looked like I had caught a little goldfish in the water, but it was talking to me. As I looked closer, I could see it wasn't a goldfish. It was a wee little golden mermaid, and she knew my name. She was adorable, about as big as my pinkie, and gold from the top of her head to the tip of her glittering tail.

"Hello, Vivian," she said in a whispery voice. "My name is Goldie. I have been waiting for you to catch me for a very long time. Do not be afraid of me. I am going to be your secret friend for the rest of your life. Please don't tell anybody about me. It might break the spell of your being able to see and hear me. I love your sandcastle. Your moat gives me a wonderful place to swim and keep you company today. Please, dump me into the water and we'll have a nice visit, just the two of us."

My mommy and daddy had read me stories from picture books about mermaids, but I never dreamed I would have a real live mermaid friend to play with at the beach. That was our first day together, and listening to Goldie was much better than my picture book stories. She told me magical tales about her adventures and treasures in the sea living with her mermaid family. To my surprise she wanted to know all about my life and what I did with my legs and feet. She was very interested in what my life was like without the ocean to live in.

The day flew by, and Goldie knew that I'd soon be called to go home. She said, "Lean in real close. I want to tell you how we can be together forever." First she told me to go find the biggest Conch shell on the beach and bring it to her. Then she said, "Close your eyes now so I can magically swim into the shell and be safe." When I opened my eyes, Goldie was gone, but I could hear her calling my name from inside the shell. "Vivian, will you please put this shell in your beautiful pail and take me home with you? Always keep the shell in a very safe place. Any time you are alone and want to be with me again, just pick up the shell and put it to your ear.'"

That was the beginning of a lifelong friendship that grew and changed as we did. Goldie and I were destined to grow up and old together. When we were young, we were great playmates and best friends. As I became a young woman, she became a more intimate friend, confidant, and guardian angel. Today she is all those things, along with being my Muse. Now I know why she was called Goldie—not because of the gold I could see but because of her big golden heart.

> This tale is almost over now
> The pail gone for many a year
> The shell sits upon my shelf
> Goldie's made it very clear
> That when my life is over
> We will both get golden wings
> And fly away together
> To what ever-after brings.

Flamingo Challenge Haiku

Vivian Williford

Flamingo on hat
Pondering upon this and that
Come down for a chat

Vivian J. Williford, longtime retired, was a pioneer—one of the only female graphic artists of her time, a designer of maps. Now Vivian brings joy and light with her words, and one needs no north or south, no east or west to find directions to the heart. She is the epitome of the joy of living in the minute as Vivian espouses in her story The Golden Hour Clock. The rest of the Budlong Woods writers miss her dearly since she relocated.

Photo by Carol Beu